THE HERB GARDEN

CHARLES LYTE

THE OXFORD ILLUSTRATED PRESS

THE OXFORD ILLUSTRATED PRESS
ISBN 0 946609 20 9

Published by:
The Oxford Illustrated Press,
Sparkford, Near Yeovil,
Somerset BA22 7JJ, England.
Haynes Publications Inc
861 Lawrence Drive, Newbury Park, California 91320 USA.

Printed in England by:
J. H. Haynes & Co. Ltd., Sparkford, Near Yeovil, Somerset BA22 7JJ.

British Library Cataloguing in Publication Data
Lyte, Charles
   The herb garden.
   1. Herb gardening
   1. Title
   635'.7   SB351.H5

ISBN 0-946609-20-9

Library of Congress Catalog Card Number
86-81825

For my daughter, Caroline, and my Son-in-Law, John, and their first garden.

ACKNOWLEDGEMENTS

I would like to acknowledge my very great gratitude for all the help I have received in preparing this book, especially from the Chief Librarian of the Royal Horticultural Society Lindey Library, Dr. Brent Elliott, and Barbara Collecott; the Staff of the London Library; the National Trust Photographic Library; Miss Marilyn Ward, and Mr. Svanderlik Milan, of the Royal Botanic Gardens, Kew; Miss Eileen Tweedie for photographing the coloured illustrations of herbs from Woodville's Medical Botany, and the staff of the English Tourist Board Photographic Library. I am also grateful to the Executors of the W.H. Davies Estate, and the publisher, Jonathan Cape, for permission to reprint 'Flowers' from *The Complete Poems of W.H. Davies*, and to the Oxford University Press for permission to print 'Old Man' from *The Collected Poems of Edward Thomas*, Edited by F. George Thomas.

Contents

Introduction

I first became interested and actively involved with herbs when I was about eleven or twelve years old, and discovered a worm-chewed copy of *A New Herbal or Historie of Plants* by D. Rembert Dodoens, which had been translated from French into English by my seventeenth-century ancestor, Henry Lyte. Through its beautifully printed pages I plunged into a world where people suffered from such distressing ailments as blastings of the belly; corrupt and rotten matter, the laske, tenesme, and falling sickness; whose eyes were afflicted with the webbe, the pearl and the haw; whose hair and teeth were constantly falling out, along with other bits and pieces. It was a pretty nightmarish world of maladies which seemed to have been contrived by the imps of hell to torment sinners. But, for every ghastly scourge, there was a treatment; if not a cure there was something that 'comforteth' and that something was to be found growing in the garden, woods, meadows, hedgerows, ditches, swampy places, or open moorland.

While I knew that I was not qualified to diagnose whether my parents, or brothers and sister were sickening for the tertian or quartane fever, about to be consumed by St. Anthony's Fire, or were in need of a stirring of bodily lust, or alternatively having it damped down (I had discovered from this magical book that certain plants were credited with achieving these interesting effects), it did seem reasonable and kindly to try to pre-empt any ill-health among the family, or at least give them a sporting chance of survival should any of these frightful ills strike them. So I took to gathering herbs and drying them until I felt confident that my *Materia Medica* was fairly comprehensive and that the time had come to put it to good use, which I did one Sunday afternoon by offering to make the tea, adding to the Earl Grey a pinch of this and a touch of that. The effect was magnificent. They raised their cups, drank, and their faces were transformed into masks of disbelief. My father broke the silence. 'Good God, what's this?' he asked. Of course I had to confess, and was made to wash out the teapot several times, and henceforth was discouraged from making tea.

This unfortunate incident did not have the effect of putting me off herbs or growing them; they had taken a grip that was not to be loosened. A herb garden, even if in reality it is no more than a tiny bed in a town garden, a border among the vegetables, or a few plants crammed into a window box or an earthenware crock, is the living evidence of a rich story that reaches far beyond recorded history.

Still as fresh and beautiful as they were when some ancient hand stretched out and plucked, crushed and first smelt their wonderful aromas, and tasted the extraordinary variety of their flavours, the herbs we grow speak of Druids, necromancers, witches and warlocks, legends and half-forgotten rituals. But it is not only in the fanciful faerie world of spells and incantations, and quaint beliefs, that herbs have played such a central role; medicine, cookery, cosmetics, dyes, human and animal health all in their various ways have, and still do, depend on herbs.

Even now research and the constant quest for cures and treatments for such devastating diseases as cancer, look to plants – herbs – to reinforce the armoury against illness. At the Royal Botanic Gardens at Kew in London, and at similar centres throughout this country and the rest of the world, scientists are constantly searching through millions of dried specimens of plants in herbariums for material which might hold the key to some new breakthrough.

Of course many of the species being examined by scientists come from tropical countries and can have no place in our temperate climate, but we are still left with a range of herb plants that will thrive and add great beauty and interest to our gardens. There is a natural enough tendency to believe that by herbs one really means mint and parsley, sage, thyme and perhaps fennel and dill, but these important culinary herbs are merely a pinch of savour compared with the huge pot-pourri of scent and flavour available to the grower.

The decline into which herbs sank during the latter part of the nineteenth century and the early part of this century has been halted, and in fact reversed by an adventurous and widespread interest in them both for cooking and alternative medicine which is bringing about a remarkable renaissance for these wonderful plants.

It strikes me that there is a mistaken belief that to retain the purity of the art of herb growing they must be cultivated in the classical herb garden with its small beds, intersecting paths, perhaps borders of dwarf box hedges, which, incidently are safe and cosy quarters for slugs and snails. If you have the space such gardens are entirely charming, but the fact is that herbs can be grown just about anywhere; odd corners of the kitchen garden, between cracks in paving stones, in pots on the kitchen window-shelf. They will flourish in the herbaceous border, and, indeed, those such as clary sage, elecampane and woad have been moved from practical use to decorative. In the shrubbery, woodland and wild garden, even in the grass, they take their place with grace and a very special kind of beauty.

Grown in a border on their own they lend colour and form, as well as being useful. The blues, pinks, reds, white and yellows, and the shades and tones of green, purple and gold serve to remind us of medieval tapestries and paintings. Herbs do not have the unfortunate garishness of so many modern hybrid ornamental plants, instead there is a sublety of colour that shares easily the marvellous fragrance that a hand brushed through the foliage will release.

As if they were not sufficient in themselves, it is not only the practical and aesthetic quality of herbs that is irresistible, it is also their history, lore and legend. They are tied so closely to the saga of mankind, that inevitably their story is quite as arresting and extraordinary as that of the men and women they have served.

In this book I hope that I will be able to share my pleasure and delight in herbs. I fear you will discover little about the mechanical process of growing the plants; there are so many how-to-do-it books already on the market that I doubt whether I could do more than act the part of the chorus. In my experience, given well-husbanded soil the majority of herbs will do very well without too much coddling. They don't seek show-bench fame.

So really this is a journey from the past to the present, with a lot of side-tracking into neolithic villages, Roman feasts, medieval banquets; into monastery gardens and cottages, kitchens and druid's glades; the sometimes dotty, star-struck teaching of Culpeper, to our own time. It is not a meticulously mapped journey, it really can't be, but perhaps more of a Bummel, as described by Jerome K. Jerome.

'A "Bummel," I explained, 'I should describe as a journey, long or short, without an end; the only thing regulating it being the necessity of getting back within a given time to the point from which one started. Sometimes it is through busy streets, and sometimes through the fields and lanes; sometimes we can be spared for a few hours, and sometimes for a few days. But long or short, but here or there, our thoughts are ever on the running of the sand. We nod and smile to many as we pass; with some we stop and talk awhile; and with a few we walk a little way. We have been much interested, and often a little tired. But on the whole we have had a pleasant time, and we are sorry when 'tis over.'

Fortunately with herbs it is a journey of discovery that 'tis never over. They certainly have a past and a present, and undoubtedly a future, and I can't think of a time when they have let me down, in the sense of being boring.

It is a shame to end on a serious warning note, but I must offer some words of caution. In writing about the medicinal role of herbs, I have described what they were, or are supposed to cure or relieve, but no-one should experiment without seeking the advice of a qualified herbalist.

1
First Consult The Goat

It is a truism, but one that bears repeating again and again, that the animal kingdom (and that includes mankind), and the vegetable kingdom, are inextricably bound together. But there is one vital distinction, and that is that the vegetable kingdom could get along very nicely without man, while man would perish without plants. I merely point this out because, ever since the human race discovered how to exploit vegetable production in a regulated way, it has doggedly contrived to destroy those very plants, whether trees or tubers, either by over-cropping, or by mono-cropping, which seems to require the extinction of every other plant that might conceivably interfere with the primary crop, while at the same time maximising its exposure to disease and pests. Much of the destruction has appeared to be almost capricious, although the cause has often been want and need; far too often it is inspired by pure greed. The systematic felling of the rain forests for valuable timber; the grubbing up of hedgerows to create economic and profitable prairie-style fields; the profligate use of herbicides, insecticides, and artificial fertilisers; all these activities and many more have placed a hideous strain on the vegetable kingdom.

It is not a modern phenomenon, although it has intensified in recent decades. The great forests once covering vast areas of Britain were cut for building and fuel. The miracle is that there is still such an abundance of plant species surviving – but the tragedy is that we shall never know, particularly as far as the rain forests are concerned, what has been lost for all time.

Despite what may have been lost through the refinements of modern scientific detection, the palaeobotanists have been able to reveal a great deal about the plant foods gathered and eaten by very ancient peoples. They have been able to identify the seeds of food plants in graves, impressed on pottery shards, in the middens of prehistoric settlements, and in the layers of soil and rubble that are carefully removed and sifted by archaeologists. The evidence has been dredged from shipwrecks, found in fossils, even in the ashes of cooking fires and burned buildings. Most of the discoveries have been of fruits and vegetables which made up the daily diet, according to the season (or even of those out of season, as in the case of pulses and cereals, which were dried and stored). However, alongside those vegetables which were clearly grown and harvested for everyday survival, a considerable number of remains of plants (now regarded as weeds) have been found in archeological sites, and while they were probably never cultivated, it does seem likely they were gathered for food or medicine, or both.

The contents of the stomach of the Tollund Man, almost perfectly preserved after 2000 years in a Danish peat bog, included seeds of dock, bindweed and chamomile. Other seeds found by palaeobotanists include couch grass, shepherd's purse, fat hen, plantain and chickweed, and a number of the wild precursors of our familiar modern vegetables. Certainly chickweed was a popular salad vegetable until relatively recent times, but were the other 'weeds' simply a source of greenstuff, or were they eaten for their real or imagined health-giving qualities? What is interesting is the fact that all the plants that were obviously used by prehistoric people are to be found in herbals, where they are recommended for the treatment of diseases, ill-health and injury.

On the sites of the Swiss Lake Dwellers' settlements archaeologists have found opium poppy seeds, and evidence to suggest that they were used medicinally, probably to relieve pain.

Herbs still used by American Indians have been discovered among the remains of very old Indian villages.

Scientists believe that prehistoric people made use of herbs as purgatives and emetics, and also used plant material to treat wounds.

It has been proved that animals are instinctive herbalists, and it is perfectly reasonable to suppose that in the first place man discovered curative herbs by watching sick animals treat themselves. Anyone who keeps a dog or a cat will have seen how they will eat couch-grass to induce vomiting, thus voiding some impurity. Goats have always had a reputation for being particularly talented at seeking out physic herbs. Ailing sheep will hunt for dandelions. In India monkeys have been observed pulling splinters from themselves and other monkeys, and then covering the wounds with pads of leaves, and in troops of Baboons, biologists believe that one animal is appointed as the community's physician.

Balm and borage, aniseed, dill, chicory, fennel, hyssop and horehound, rosemary, rue, marjoram, sorrel, tansy, sage and yarrow are herbs that animals willingly feed upon, and they all have medicinal properties. Veterinary herbalists recommend growing these plants in hedgerows where browsing animals can reach them.

So by watching what the animals they hunted fed on, ancient man discovered what he could eat, and what would keep him healthy. It was a cruel irony that he watched wild goats grazing on thyme or sage, or the wild mints, and then discovered they were the perfect seasoning for the animal's roast flesh!

Cultivation in those days, so far as it went, was extremely crude: virgin soil was superficially broken up with horn and stone adzes, and seeds shoved into holes made with a planting stick. Sadly such primitive methods are still to be seen – although metal has taken the place of stone and horn – in many third-world countries, particularly those constantly plagued by drought. Primitive man, like too many tribal people today, simply hunted, gathered, scratched a crop from the soil, and moved on.

It was not until groups of people settled and built reasonably permanent dwellings, that the skills of husbandry began to develop; a slow, and doubtless painful and disaster-ridden process stretched over many thousands of years. But more than five thousand years ago in India, Egypt and Mesopotamia, the arts of cultivation had arrived at a high level of perfection, and certainly by 2000 BC, in the Shantung area of China the same scene was being enacted.

Irrigation, the careful selection of plants, collecting from the wild, and the exchange of species and cultivars with similarly advanced societies, produced a remarkably varied vegetable diet in civilisations flourishing many centuries ago. It was a diet in which herbs held a dominant position, both in the kitchen and the pharmacy. They were also greatly valued for their scents and aromas. Elaborate mixtures were prepared to enhance beauty, and beat off the withering effects of age. Inevitably herbs were also drawn into the mysteries of religion, and the more sinister underworld of magic and occultism.

For the Druids, whose ministry was far wider spread than is generally understood, they provided the seven sacred plants: mistletoe, vervain, henbane, primrose, pulsatilla, clover and wolf's-bane. All remained in the *Materia Medica*.

There is something quite cosmopolitan about herbs. They might not have chosen to travel, but conquerors and colonizers alike have taken their herbs with them, and for that at least we in Britain have cause to be grateful to those who have invaded us.

2
Of Liquamen and Metheglin

The Romans, who cheerfully plundered the secrets of Greek cuisine, and no doubt that of any other country they occupied, developed cookery to a fine and intricate art. To achieve the kind of perfection they sought, they depended heavily on herbs and spices, which they not only grew with considerable skill, but also imported. It has been argued that so much money was spent on importing herbs and spices that this contributed substantially to the decline of the Empire. It is an extraordinary notion that a great civilisation should eat itself into bankruptcy, but a distinct possibility, since it is said that Apicius, the great Roman master of food and cookery, committed suicide rather than face starvation (at least starvation in his terms), when he discovered he was down to his last ten million sesterces. He had already spent one hundred million sesterces on satisfying his elaborate tastes.

Strong flavours were particularly sought in Roman cookery, which was why herbs, such as rue and lovage were essential ingredients. The arsenal of herbs used in the Roman kitchen reads exactly like the list of any well-stocked herb border in a modern garden: fennel and dill, hyssop, savory, saffron, cumin, coriander, chervil, costmary, thyme, mint, parsley, bay, oregano, caraway, myrtle, mustard, borage, southernwood, sweet marjoram, sweet cicely, sage, poppy seed, wormwood, garlic and pennyroyal. Celery was grown primarily for its seeds, and elecampane, which was to become much more important as a medicinal herb, was cultivated for its roots and leaves, which were used in cooking. In addition, of course, there were the imported spices.

Herbs and spices were used in combination with equally power-fully flavoured ingredients such as liquamen, made from the fermented entrails of fish, and special wines which tended to be sweet and syrupy. In the case of many dishes, the meat and vegetables were cooked in highly seasoned stocks or water, and brought to the table with rich sauces. Indeed, when one reads the recipes that have been handed down by Apicius, scarcely a single dish was served without a redolent, herby dressing. Take, for example, elaeologarum sauce that went with snails; it was made from lovage, coriander, rue, oil and fish stock.

With the collapse of the Roman Empire, the consequent loss to the formerly subject nations of direct Roman influence, and the restoration, in many cases, of barbarism, it would not have been altogether surprising if the knowledge of herbs and their cultivation had disap-peared. But this was not the case, although both use and cultivation were generally confined to relatively few places.

The great Frankish leader, Charlemagne, who succeeded his father Pippin III in 768 AD, took a close interest in gardening, including the cultivation of herbs. It is amazing that he was able to do so, since almost all of his forty-six year reign was occupied with warfare and conquest; yet as he swept the Moors out of Europe, and established the Pyrenees as a rampart against Spain; brought the Gauls to heel, introduced Christianity to Bavaria, and dismissed the Lombards from Italy, he found time to turn his thoughts to gardening. It was on his specific orders that chicory, clary, fennel, iris (for its rhizomes), mallows, mints, poppy, rosemary, rue, sage, savory, southernwood, tansy, bay, agrimony and betony were always to be found in his gardens.

Early in the ninth century the plan for the ideal monastery garden was drawn up for the foundation of St. Gall in Switzerland. It was on a grand scale, but it was also intended as a model for other religious houses. For example, the physic garden was to have sixteen beds instead of the normal four, and they were to be stocked with beans (used both as food and medicine), savory, roses, horse mint, cumin, lovage, fennel, tansy, costmary, lilies, sage, rue, flag irises, pennyroyal, fenugreek, mint and rosemary. Parsley and coriander, chervil, dill, poppy and savory were grown in the kitchen garden.

St. Gall did serve as a broad blueprint for monasteries, but at an average foundation one would have found all the physic herbs being grown in four beds in the Herbarium or Herbularius, close to the doctor monk's house. Culinary herbs were with the vegetables in the Hortus, the kitchen garden. Because they were to a great extent protected from the rigours of the outside world, monks were left in peace to cultivate their land and keep alive the skills of gardening. Through exchanges and visits to and from foreign orders, many new plants were established in Britain.

The use of herbs for treating illness and injury, and indeed in almost all areas of domestic life, spread out from the religious houses to the laity. In the thirteenth century John Garlande was listing in his works essential plants for the garden: sage, parsley, dittany, hyssop, celandine, fennel, pellitory, columbine, roses, lilies, violets, nettles and thistles, and specifically for medicine: mercury, mallow, agrimony, nightshade and chicory – all plants that would have been grown by monks and nuns.

There seems at first glance to have been a curious muddling and merging of herbs used for both pot and pharmacy. The fact is that the line between medicinal and cooking herbs was so fine as often hardly to exist at all. After the long winter and the lean days of early spring, existing on a poor diet of stale pulses and cereals, and the last of the root vegetables and salt meat, the sense of well-being, to say nothing of clearing the unpleasant symptoms of scurvy, gave most greenstuff a medicinal and curative reputation which was not always justified.

Medieval gardening saw herbs in a pre-eminent position. The doctor monks, the Infirmarers and the nursing sisters, particularly those of the Benedictine Order, cultivated at least one hundred different herbs in their gardens, and, indeed, Anglo-Saxon herbalists listed as many as five hundred, although many of these would have been plants gathered from the wild, rather than cultivated.

As the medieval period became more settled and great estates were developed, so gardens were planted. Herb growing was no longer restricted to religious houses. Orchards were cultivated, not for their fruits alone, but also as pleasure grounds, and plots of herbs were set about the orchards to add scents to the beauty of the scene; herbs such as rue, sage, basil, combined with violets, columbine, lilies, roses and irises. The plants now associated with flower borders were then used in cooking, perfumery and medicine.

More intimate than the orchards were the walled and locked herb gardens, where the emphasis was on scented and aromatic plants, such as basil, lavender, marjoram, savory, mint, caraway and coriander. Sweet scents were greatly valued in medieval times, and before a feast the guests would wash their hands in herb-scented water, while angelica seeds were burnt to perfume the room. The scented water was made with rose leaves, thyme, lavender, sage, camomile, marjoram and orange peel, sometimes used separately, or as mixtures.

The floors were strewn, not only with *acorus*, the sweet rush, but with a variety of herbs, including balm, marjoram, mint, lavender, sage, fennel, hyssop, camomile, costmary, cowslips, germander, violets, tansy, and the leaves of our native wild strawberry. The great Elizabethan, Francis Bacon, believed that the aroma of wilting strawberry leaves acted as a cordial.

Like Roman cookery, medieval cuisine was dominated by herbs, from the thick pottages to the sauces for a remarkable array of meats ranging from rabbits and chickens, to seagulls, bustards, porpoises, seals, indeed, just about anything that flew, ran or swam was likely to end up at a medieval banquet. These great, lengthy events were magnificent, luxurious and as intricate in manners and ceremony as they were in the preparation of the many dishes, which were invariably concluded with an assortment of sweetmeats, whose ingredients included roses, anise, fennel, coriander, sage and saffron.

Much of what was served would today seem at least strange, if not disgusting. For instance a **Medieval Custard** would come as a remarkable shock: veal was cut into small pieces, washed and boiled with parsley, sage, savory and hyssop, all finely chopped. When the mixture was boiling, ground pepper, cinnamon, cloves, mace and saffron were added. Once the veal was well cooked it was removed and the cooled liquid was thickened into a custard with beaten eggs. The meat was made into pies with chopped dates, powdered ginger, verjuice, the custard and baked in pastry cases.

As well as wine, metheglin would have been served. It was a favourite drink of the time made from boiling up herbs with water and fermented honey.

Less surprising would have been the **Salads**, which were a feature of even quite simple meals. One might be composed of water-cress, onions, leeks, lettuce, mint, sorrel, and other available fresh herbs. It would be sprinkled with vinegar, verjuice or wine. In another you would find parsley, sage, garlic, chiboules or shallots, onions, leeks, borage, cresses, rue, rosemary and purslane, all seasoned with salt and vinegar. Calamint, primroses and chickweed were also used.

The favourite medieval culinary herbs, particularly in French cooking, were tansy, rue, pennyroyal and hyssop. These very strong flavours were chosen as a match for the meats, which were mainly game, and certainly gamey. This preference for powerful tastes was reflected in the most popular herb seeds used in the cooking of the time; caraway, mustard, cardamom, coriander and cumin.

The potherb garden would certainly have included borage, bugloss, violets, mallows, mercury, dandelion, avence, mint, sage, parsley, marigolds, marjoram, fennel, caraway, red nettle, clary, daisies, chervil, thyme, betony, columbine, basil, dill, dittany and harts tongue. And there would have been fenugreek, costmary, southernwood, cumin, tarragon, anise, lovage, summer savory, feverfew, houseleek, camomile and comfrey. Some of these, such as feverfew, southernwood and camomile are inconceivable as culinary herbs now, but then they were probably added to pottages as a general aid to health.

For distilling, either for medicine or perfume, the gardeners were expected to cultivate red roses, rosemary, dragans (Herb Serpentine), scabious, eye-bright, wormwood, mugweed, betony, tansy, sage, hyssop and ersemart. One distillation, which was certainly still being made in the seventeenth century, was Plague Water. A handful each of rosemary, balm, borage, angelica, carduus, celandine, tarragon, feverfew, wormwood, pennyroyal, elecampane roots, mugwort, bural, tormentil, agrimony, sage and sorrel were put into four quarts of white wine. The container was closed and stood in a cellar for nine days, after which the infusion was distilled.

3

Witchcraft and Wisdom

Throughout most of the fifteenth century, England was racked by civil war, and this had the effect of setting back any real advances in gardening, but once the Tudors had consolidated their power, following their triumph at the Battle of Bosworth in 1485, there was a renewed interest in the culture of plants, not least of all, herbs.

Medical practice was still dominated by the works of the ancients, led by Dioscorides, and Pliny the Elder's huge *History of the World*, which was commonly known as 'The Natural History'.

Dioscorides of Anazarba in Cilicia compiled his great herbal during the first century AD. He was a professional soldier, who had travelled widely, and had had the opportunity to collect information, and, indeed, to observe many of the plants he wrote about, at first hand. For one thousand, five hundred years it was the main source book for physicians, but it was not translated from the Greek into English until 1655. The task was undertaken by John Goodyer, but the book remained in manuscript form gathering dust in Magdalen College Library for centuries, until the Oxford University Press published it in 1934.

Pliny's book, on the other hand, was published in 1634, after being translated into English by Philemon Holland, a Doctor of Physicke. It undoubtedly influenced thinking and practice. He constructed this remarkable work from a combination of observation and a great deal of hearsay. The use of herbs ranged from the sensible, safe, and probably useful, to the positively dangerous. Whilst warning that it is toxic, he nevertheless recommended mandrake as an aid to sleep. Dioscorides said that the leaves should be eaten, despite the fact that they are poisonous.

Certainly Pliny's herbal cures were generally a great deal less hazardous and repelling than those based on animal products. People suffering from depression and lethargy should, he advised, be dosed with calves dung, boiled in wine. The prospect of the medicine would surely have been enough to bring on a bout of depression. The same mixture was used to remove warts from a donkey's leg. Sleeping sickness was treated with wolf's liver boiled in wine, while consumptives were urged to inhale the smoke from burning cow's dung.

And so the concoctions go on. Ashes of pig's dung in new wine; the lungs of a red deer; boar's urine; scrapings from a stag's skin mixed with vinegar, or the foam from a boar's muzzle whipped up with vinegar. The blood of baby weazles was used in a revolting brew to counteract poisoned draughts and sorcery; slug's heads were worn as a necklace to cure a headache. Cures for baldness were pretty unsavoury. Ashes of sheep's dung worked up into a paste with honey and oil; mouse droppings, and the burnt bodies of mice and flies, rubbed into the scalp; burnt lizards mixed with onions and bear's grease; hen's dung and raven's eggs, or burnt viper's skins. With cures like that it is surprising that people didn't just opt for baldness or a wig.

Herbal medicine in Britain was not solely in the hands of scholars and the clergy. The Welsh herbal doctors, known at the Meddygion Myddfai, were a laity with a long tradition, which was only broken in 1842, when the last of them died, taking their secrets with him. As befits a land which produced Merlin, they claimed a magical origin. According to the legend there was once, in the distant past, a cowherd living near a village called Llanddeusant, who fell in love with a water nymph. After courting her for a considerable period she agreed to marry him, but warned that if he struck her three times she would return to the lake of her birth, Llyn-y-Fan. They married and raised three sons, and although the marriage was a happy one, over the years the cowherd did hit her from time to time. On the third occasion she disappeared. Once she did reappear, and that was to tell her eldest son that he and his male descendants would become great doctors; she gave him a sack of herbs to get him started. He had three sons, and it is claimed that they wrote a book containing nine hundred herbal recipes.

That particular herbal appears to have vanished like the water nymph who started it all, but from the early years of the sixteenth century there was a fairly steady flow of new herbals. In 1516 a French work, *The Great Herbal*, was published in English, followed by a translation from the Latin of *The Little Herbal* in 1525. Between 1540 and 1550, the *Book of the Properties of Herbs* by Cary; Macer's *Herbal*, and the *Little Herbal* by Ascham, appeared.

William Turner's great *Herbal*, often regarded as the first important English work, came out in 1551. Henry Lyte's translation of Dodoen's herbal, to which he added from his own research and scholarship, followed in 1578, and was a very popular and authoritative work, only displaced in 1597 by John Gerard's *The Herbal or General Historie of Plantes*, which remained unassailed for forty-three years, when John Parkinson published the *Theatre of Plants*. Thirteen years later Nicholas Culpeper had his herbal published.

It has to be said that most of the authors borrowed heavily from the writings of the ancients, and from one another's work, but the sixteenth and seventeenth centuries did see the beginnings of a more scientific approach to herbal medicine, although it was still subject to a good deal of mysticism and folk-wisdom.

The Doctrine of Signatures went virtually unchallenged, and was the basis for many herbal treatments. The theory was that the curative plants revealed themselves, either growing at the source of some scourge, or through a distinguishing colour or shape. The herbalists saw an even-handedness in the divine arrangement, whereby disease and injury were dished out with one hand, and the cure with the other, thus willow was used to treat fevers and ague, because it grew in swamps and boggy places, which were suspected of being the cause of the disorders.

Equally, Lesser Celandine was used to dose people suffering from jaundice because of its yellow flowers, and its roots, which form clusters of tiny tubers were used in the treatment of piles because they look remarkably like haemorrhoids. Whether it is a happy coincidence or not, many of the Doctrine of Signatures herbs did bring relief to those stricken by the twinned ailments.

Astro-herbalism – the linking of plants to astrological signs was always popular, and given some kind of scientific credence, however spurious, by Nicholas Culpeper. In fact the belief still enjoys some currency to this day. Here the theory is that all parts of the body, head – throat, hands, arms, heart, lungs, liver, kidneys, sex organs, legs etc. – have an astrological sign and a ruling planet. If, for example, something goes wrong with the liver, which comes under Sagittarius, and whose ruling planet is Jupiter, then you treat it with a plant under the influence of Jupiter. Astro-herbalism was greatly favoured by the ancient scholars, as well as sorcerers and witches, the latter, of course, engaging in even more bizarre beliefs and rituals.

There were those who practiced Botanomacy, divination through plants; plants such as soapwort, dwarf elder and sweet cicely were particularly valued if they grew in churchyards; dew collected from fennel, greater and lesser celandine, lady's mantle and sundew, was supposed to contain special and powerful medicinal properties.

The gathering of herbs often involved elaborate and uncomfortable rituals. Usually you had to go alone and secretly, very often at night, naked, or at least barefoot. Sometimes it was necessary to approach a plant backwards. To complicate matters even further, it was held that herbs had temperaments; they were either hot, cold, moist, dry or temperate. This is how Culpeper explained it:

'The qualities of medicine are considered in respect of men, not of themselves; for these simples are called hot, which heat our bodies; those cold, which cool them; and those temperate which work no change at all in them, in respect of either heat, cold, dryness, or moisture. And these may be temperate, as being neither hot nor cold; yet, may be moist or dry; or being neither moist nor dry, yet may be hot or cold: or, lastly, being neither hot, cold, moist, nor dry.

'In temperature there is no degree of difference; the difference of the other qualities are divided into four degrees, beginning at temperature; so that a medicine may be said to be hot, cold, moist, or dry, in the first, second, third, or fourth degree.'

A number of plants, which had magical associations in pre-Christian times, were later named in honour of the Virgin Mary: Lady's Smock, Lady's Bedstraw, Lungwort (which is also known as Mary's

Milkdrops), and Lady's Tears (Lily-of-the-Valley). In Ireland St. John's Wort is known as Mary's Sweat, from the belief that it sprang from the drops of sweat she shed whilst in labour during the birth of Christ. St. John's Wort is the principal plant connected with St. John's Eve (June 23), which was a date prominent in the pagan calendar. In the more recent past it was an evening of great significance among country people, and the shades of its much earlier history were quite evident. Fires were lit on the hilltops to protect people and animals from any malevolent spirits, and to ensure a year free from the influence of the dark forces of the supernatural. In addition a number of particularly powerful protective plants were dried in the fires to both preserve them, and fill them with the potency of the flames, so that they could be worn as a defensive amulet for the remainder of the year.

St. John's Wort was the most important of the plants preserved by the fires. The others were ivy, mugwort, yarrow, vervain, orpine, yellow iris, elder, figwort, white campion, bladder campion, foxglove, wild thyme, fennel, melilot, ox-eye, camomile, corn marigold, dodder, plantain, Jack-go-to-bed-at-noon, hawthorn, lime blossom, lavender, quaking grass, and male fern.

Despite the myth and mystery that still existed, the Tudors were clearly anxious to sweep away at least some of the old ignorance. In his dedication to Queen Elizabeth of his translation of Dodoens, Henry Lyte, albeit somewhat fulsomely, expresses something of the current thinking:

'. . . we thinke no travell (labour) too great, whereby we are in hope both to profit our Country, and to please so noble and loving a Princesse, whose whole power and endevour we see thereto bent, that vertue and knowledge (the two most beautiful ornaments of a well gouverned Kingdome) may flourish and beare sway: vice and ignorance (the foes of all goodnes) may vanish and give place.'

They were also well aware that including herbs in their diet, not only made the food taste better, but also induced good health.

Queen Elizabeth used to breakfast off a soup made from an old hen, a young cock, a handful of parsley, a sprig of thyme, three sprigs of spearmint, a small quantity of balm, half an onion, pepper, salt, and a clove. The ingredients were covered with water and the liquid boiled down to less than a pint.

As in medieval times, salads continued to dominate the Tudor table, and they were rich in herbs and flowers. Marigolds (known simply as golds), violets and primroses, were added to give colour and scent. John Evelyn, in his remarkable book, *Acetaria. A Discourse on Sallets*, published at the very end of the seventeenth century, urged the use of herbs, and wayside plants, in a daily salad. While salads remained popular, towards the close of the seventeenth century there was a move, particularly in French cooking, away from the medieval vogue for the excessive use of herbs and spices. The bouquet garni was taking over. One such was a piece of bacon in a bundle with scallions, thyme, cloves, chervil and parsley. A popular dried mixture was parsley, sage, winter savory, thyme, marjoram, hyssop, marigold petals and basil.

The practice of making food into a kind of combined dish and dose was fading away, and the distinction between physic and culinary herbs was becoming clearer.

4

Behind the Stable

The eighteenth century brought enormous changes to British gardening with the arrival of the fashion for landscape design which, despite the magnificence of its results, destroyed virtually all of the traditional medieval and Tudor gardens. It was a ruthless exercise, although its architects were convinced, as were their patrons, that their work was constructive rather than destructive. Labyrinths and mazes, parterres and knot gardens, archery butts, bowling greens, jousting yards, and mounts were swept away by men like William Kent, Lancelot 'Capability' Brown, and Humphrey Repton. They thought nothing of levelling a hamlet or altering the course of a river to flood a valley and create a lake.

Needless to say the lovely old herb gardens were among their victims, and the plants themselves were relegated to the kitchen garden, which in turn was hidden away, preferably, according to Philip Miller, the great curator of the Chelsea Physic Garden in that century, somewhere behind the stables so as to be out of sight, and conveniently close at hand to a ready supply of manure.

Only Batty Langley seems to have considered that the herb garden had the right to a place of its own in the eighteenth-century scheme of things. In his *New Principles of Gardening*, published in 1728, he described his perfect garden. It was a fussy and extraordinary collection of meadows, coppices, ruins, rocks and grottos, haystacks and forest trees. Somewhere amidst all this he wanted a herb or physic garden. But really it was only to be part of a whimsical decoration.

Even if the herb gardens themselves were out of fashion, herbs themselves were not.

Medicine was still dominated by herbs, and the simpling women made their living by scouring the hedgerows, meadows and woods for material for the herbalists. As a boy, the great eighteenth-century naturalist and explorer, Sir Joseph Banks, was taught his early botany by these women working around Eton, where he was at school. While it might no longer apply to the daughters of wealthy families, for country women the knowledge of growing and using herbs was still regarded as one of the highest of the female graces. Grandmothers and mothers passed on the secrets of twig-runes, the herbal cures, to the young girls. The early settlers in New England took 'weeds' with them, like yarrow and dandelions, chickweed, buttercup and shepherd's purse, to treat their sick. As late as the early 1900s, eighty per cent of all medicines were derived from roots, barks and leaves.

In the sixth edition of *The Gardeners Dictionary*, Philip Miller lists no less than 260 medicinal plants, and 27 large trees considered to have medicinal properties. He goes so far as to describe where many of the herbs can be found growing in the wild so that his readers could collect them and grow them in their gardens. Interestingly he describes *Canabis sativa* as an English plant, and said it was to be found growing on dunghills; no doubt having escaped from the fields where it was grown commercially to produce hemp for cordage.

Self-help medicine was still practised in the majority of homes. Mrs. Hannah Glasse who, according to an exchange in Boswell's *Life of Johnson*, was in fact a Dr. Hill, urges housewives to make **Plague Water**, and gives the recipe in 'The Art of Cookery Made Plain and Easy'. Take a handful each of rue, sage, mint, rosemary, wormwood and lavender. Infuse in a gallon of white wine vinegar. Pour into a stone jar, seal and keep in warm ashes for four days. Strain and bottle in quart bottles with an ounce of camphor in each bottle. Use it as a daily mouth wash, rub on loins and temples, and sniff a little up the nostrils. Also carry a sponge impregnated with the mixture to sniff if close to anyone suffering from the plague. There was a story current in 1755, when the book was published, of a gang of four robbers who broke into infected houses, murdered the occupants and stole the valuables. They confessed on the gallows that they used the mixture to protect themselves from infection.

Tonic drinks were also popular, such as **Seed Water**, which was made by bruising a spoonful of coriander, and half a spoonful of caraway seeds, and boiling them in a pint of water. The liquid was strained off, beaten up with an egg yolk, and mixed with sherry and sugar.

Apart from medicinal herbs, Miller's Dictionary also describes all the familiar culinary herbs in some detail, with instruction on how to grow them. What is missing is any real dissertation on herb gardens. Mawe and Abercrombie, in *Every Man his Own Gardener*, one of the most popular practical gardening books of the eighteenth century, set out a list of essential sweet and pot-herbs. They were: double and single marigolds, winter and summer savory, sweet and pot marjoram, common, lemon and silver-tipped thyme, common and variegated hyssop, red, green, tea and balsamic sage, spearmint, peppermint and orange mint, balm, pennyroyal, double camomile, fennel, dill, lavender, rosemary, sweet and bush basil, anise, caraway, orach, clary, borage, salad burnet, tarragon, buglos, carduus benedictus and cat mint.

British cooking in the eighteenth century had a poor name with foreign visitors. They were daunted by the endless pies and puddings, huge joints of meat, and mounds of dreary-looking vegetables dripping in butter. But one wonders whether it was a fair picture. Many eighteenth-century recipes declare a highly imaginative use of herbs and flavourings. **Stewed Rump of Beef** sounds as though it could be pretty grim, but not cooked this way. Boil a rump of beef until it is about half cooked, remove from the liquid and skin. Take salt, pepper, beaten mace, grated nutmeg, a handful of parsley, a little thyme, winter savory and sweet marjoram. Chop the herbs finely, and mix with the salt and spices. Make large holes in the joint and stuff them with the herb mixture, keeping enough back to mix with the yolks of two eggs. Spread the mixture over the meat. Mix the juices which have run out of the joint with a pint of claret, and pour over the rump. Bake in a deep pan for two hours or however long it takes to cook the meat through. Serve with the liquid.

Green Sauce was a great favourite of the century, and it could be made in a number of ways. One was to take two handfuls of sorrel pounded in a mortar (or nowadays, liquidised). Press out the juice, heat in a saucepan with liquid butter, add sugar and the juice of a lemon. Another was to pound or liquidise two handfuls of sorrel and two pippins cut into quarters. Squeeze out the juice and add the juice of a lemon, or the equivalent quantity of vinegar. Sweeten with sugar. Green sauce can be eaten with fish or poultry.

Tripe is delicious, but too frequently it is served floundering about in a swamp of boiled milk and onions. In the eighteenth century it was often roasted. The tripe was cut into two square pieces, and a stuffing of breadcrumbs, pepper, salt, nutmeg, sweet herbs, lemon peel and egg yolks, was spread on the fat side of one square. The other square was laid on top, fat side down, forming a sandwich, which was rolled, tied, basted with butter and roasted.

Roast Pigeons were stuffed with fresh chopped parsley, or served with a thick sauce made from finely chopped parsley, butter and vinegar.

A dish, which could have come straight out of a modern book of supper recipes, was **Herby Eggs:** take two cabbage leaves and scald them with mushrooms, parsley, sorrel and chervil, and chop them small with hard-boiled egg yolks; season with salt and nutmeg, cook in butter. Cover the bottom of a dish with cream, pour in the mixture, and decorate the edge of the dish with finely chopped egg whites, parsley, and a powdering of salt and nutmeg. Brown under the grill.

And this **Eighteenth-Century Salad** could be part of the nouvelle cuisine: cook fresh green beans until tender, but crisp. Arrange on a dish and surround with salad burnet, chives, chervil, tarragon and parsley, all chopped small and tossed in a little vinegar, oil and ground black pepper.

Herbs featured even more prominently in French eighteenth-century cooking, particularly in simple, but delicious **Herb Soups**, such as this one in which chopped chervil, purslane, sorrel, lettuce and a little celery, were added to a grated carrot and parsnip, and cooked in a rich veal stock.

Or **Spring Porridge**, a thick broth. Take a pint of green or dried peas, chervil, purslane, lettuce, sorrel, three or four onions, and a knob of butter. Boil slowly until the vegetables and herbs are soft, strain and liquidise. Beat up six egg yolks, or as many or as few as necessary, depending on the quantity of liquid, in a quarter of the soup. Add to the remainder and heat. Put a thick slice of bread in each soup bowl, and serve.

Breast of Lamb is one of the cheapest cuts of meat, and quite delicious if well cooked. Two hundred years ago in France they would bone it, stew until tender, drain, dry and cover with a mixture of sweet herbs – marjoram, savory, chervil, parsley and basil – and grill.

They also had a way with **Sheep's Trotters**. Remove the bones and boil the trotter until tender, and then stuff the cavity with basil. Cover with egg and breadcrumbs, and fry.

Two eighteenth-century French herby fish recipes, which have the virtue of simplicity, are mussel fritters and stewed gudgeon. For **Mussel Fritters**, take the mussels out of their shells, and marinade in vinegar, water, a little butter rolled in flour, salt, pepper, chopped parsley, scallions, tarragon, garlic, a little carrot and parsnip, thyme, bay and basil.

The mixture should be lukewarm. After two hours take out the mussels, dry them, dip them in a batter made with flour, white wine, a spoonful of oil, and salt, and fry them.

Stewed Gudgeon or smelts: gudgeons and smelts are small fresh-water fish, which will be familiar to all anglers. Scale, gut and wipe clean. (Sprats and whitebait can be substituted, and will not need scaling and gutting.) Put finely chopped parsley, scallions, mushrooms, two shallots, thyme, bay and basil in a shallow dish. Season the fish on both sides and lay them on the bed of herbs. Pour over a glass of red wine, and cook until half the liquid has disappeared.

While the great landowners and their landscape architects were able to transform vast areas of the British countryside, they could not, however much they humbled them, banish the herbs from their vital place in society, even if they did have to be grown behind the stables.

5

Herbs and Their Uses
A Faggot of Herbs and Wow Wow
Sauce

It is easy and understandable to confine herbs to the kitchen and the sick-room, but in reality they have an astonishing range of uses, from a charming one of making the leaves of sweet-smelling herbs (which retain their scent after drying), into book marks, to dyes, cosmetics, wines, cordials, teas, syrups and beers, to say nothing of sauces. However, the kitchen seems about the best place to start when looking at their uses.

In the past every kitchen had its faggots of herbs. These were bundles of dried rosemary, thyme, savory and mint, which were used to flavour the pottage which was nearly always simmering over the fire, or as a brush for basting roasting meat and poultry. Whenever possible it is best to use fresh herbs, because then you have the advantage of the full flavour, but, as many particularly useful varieties die down in the winter, preservation is very important.

PRESERVATION

Nearly everyone has a favourite way of drying herbs. Dioscorides said that they should only be gathered for drying when the weather is clear. Then, he said, they would retain their goodness for up to three years. Roots should be harvested in the spring, or as the foliage is beginning to wither and fall; flowers before they fall; fruits when they are ripe, and seeds when they begin to dry. For extracting juices, he directed that the plants should be cut when they are young.

It was sound advice, which by and large has been followed for

31

centuries. Certainly herbs should be gathered when the dew is off them, and dried in a shady, airy place. If they are dried in full sunlight, much of the colour, freshness and flavour will be bleached out of them. They are supposed to dry faster if they are picked when the moon is waning, because, it is said, during that period there is less sap in the leaves and stems, and the roots are claimed to be at their tenderest when the moon is waxing. Roots, incidentally, should be cut lengthwise for drying.

Mrs. Isabella Beeton agreed that harvesting should never take place on a damp day, and should be carried out just before the plants come into flower. In *The Book of Household Management*, published in 1864, she wrote:

'It is very necessary to be particular in little matters like this, for trifles constitute perfection, and herbs nicely dried will be found very acceptable when frost and snow are on the ground. It is hardly necessary, however, to state that the flavour and fragrance of fresh herbs are incomperably finer'.

Rather like the faggots of herbs of old, she recommended drying them in small bundles, but rather than hanging them up in a shady, airy place to dry, Mrs. Beeton advised drying them quickly in an oven or in front of the fire. This was also the view of a nineteenth-century herbalist and seedsman who traded in Covent Garden, and I have certainly found that oven drying results in a greater retention of scent and flavour. Mrs. Beeton stored her bundles of herbs in paper bags, but screw-top jars, such as those that are used for instant coffee powder, are about the best storage containers. As an alternative, she suggested making a herb powder from one ounce of dried lemon thyme, one ounce of dried winter savory, one ounce of dried sweet marjoram and basil, two ounces of dried parsley, and an ounce of dried lemon peel.

Sorrel, trefoil and purslane were preserved for winter use in eighteenth-century France by washing the herbs several times, boiling in strongly salted water until all the water had disappeared, and, when cold, packing the cooked leaves in pots, which were sealed with melted butter, which was poured in when half cold. This was done in September, and the flavouring used in making soups and stuffing. Dried herbs were also infused in brandy, and used as a seasoning.

In the nineteenth century, parsley was preserved for the winter by boiling well-washed leaves for two minutes, shaking off the water, and drying rapidly in front of a fire, or in an oven. An even more ancient method of storing herbs was to press and keep them between plates of wood, but in these days of deep freezers, the simplest and best way of preserving herbs is by freezing, which also retains the greater part of their freshness. There is no need to blanch them, just wash them thoroughly, shake off the surplus water, and wrap up quantities you would normally use at any one time in clingfilm. The 'parcels' can then be put into a plastic freezer bag, and taken out as wanted.

It would be convenient if all herbs could be harvested at the same time, but this is not the case. Gathering takes place from May to September. For example: Chervil, parsley, fennel and elder flowers (May, June and July); thyme and mint (June and July); knotted marjoram, winter and summer savory (July); tarragon and salad burnet (June, July and August), and sage (August and September).

SAUCES

Herbs are essential to most sauces, and while it is a matter of personal taste, the classic sauce herbs are parsley; common, lemon and orange thyme; knotted or sweet marjoram; sage, winter savory, sweet basil, bay, tarragon, chervil and salad burnet.

Perhaps the best known of the sauces is **Parsley Sauce**, which can range from the delicious to the disastrous. The secret is to make it carefully. Wash the herb thoroughly, pick off the leaves, and boil in salted water for ten minutes. Drain very well and chop finely. Gradually mix into half a pint of melted butter. This method can be used to make sauces from chervil (a good winter substitute for parsley), basil, tarragon, salad burnet and cress. If you use flour in these sauces, make sure that it is thoroughly blended with the butter, and free from lumps.

Parsley Sauce with Liver makes an interesting sauce. Take a chicken or rabbit liver, boil for five minutes, and liquidise in a little of the liquor. Boil a decent bundle of parsley for a few minutes in salted water, shake dry, pick off the leaves, and chop finely. Mix it with the liver and a quarter of a pint of melted butter; warm, but don't boil.

Garlic Sauce: pound or liquidise two cloves of garlic with a little butter. Mix with half a pound of melted butter or beef gravy. It can also be made with garlic vinegar, and the same method can be employed substituting shallots for garlic.

Spaniards Garlic Sauce is one that can be made for keeping: slice up a pound and a half of veal or beef, season with pepper and salt, and put into a stew pan with two split carrots, four chopped cloves of garlic, a quarter of a pound of sliced ham, and a tablespoonful of water. Put on a low heat. When the meat begins to stick to the pan, turn until it is well browned. Dredge it with flour and add a quart of broth or a good stock, a bunch of sweet herbs, two bruised cloves, and a slice of lemon. Simmer for an hour and a half, skim off the fat, strain the liquid, and press out all the juices retained in the meat. It is said that this recipe was the invention of the Spaniard, who gave his name to the famous Hampstead pub, The Spaniards.

Another Spanish Sauce, also in its time known as **Brown Sauce**, but, I am happy to say, in no way related to its rather awful modern namesake, was made in a large saucepan. Take a quarter-inch thick slice of ham or bacon, and two pounds of beef or veal, a carrot, an onion stuck with four cloves, a head of celery, a bundle of parsley, lemon thyme and savory, a few leaves of basil, a bay leaf, a shallot, a piece of lemon peel, and a dozen corns of allspice. Pour on half a pint of water, cover the pot and simmer on a low heat for half an hour until almost dry. Turn the meat to brown on all sides. Add three pints of boiling water, and cook for two hours until it turns into a very rich, concentrated gravy. Use it to flavour and enrich normal gravy.

The nineteenth century saw the publication of a number of cookery books with recipes designed to inexpensively enliven the diet of the poor. While they might seem a trifle patronising, they were doubtless contrived from the finest and most altruistic motives. One was **Poor Man's Sauce**: finely chop parsley leaves and shred young green onions (spring onions will do as well). Put them in a jug with three tablespoons of oil, and five of vinegar; add black pepper and salt. Grated horseradish, or chopped pickled French beans or gherkins can be added.

Wow Wow Sauce was especially devised to go with corned beef, but since it is a fairly old recipe, corned should probably be interpreted as, silverside, although I don't see why it should not be very good with ordinary tinned corned beef. Take a good quantity of chopped parsley leaves and two or three quartered pickled cucumbers, or walnuts. Put about two ounces of butter in a pan, melt and stir in a tablespoon of flour, half a pint of beef broth, a tablespoon of vinegar, one of mushroom ketchup or port, and a teaspoon of made mustard. Simmer until thick.

Rosemary is used in a **Red Pepper Sauce**, which is made from ten tomatoes, four red peppers, one onion, a clove of garlic, salt and a large sprig of rosemary. Boil until the tomatoes are reduced to a thick pulp, and add two wine glasses of vinegar, three or four cloves, and a little cinnamon. Boil for a further ten minutes, liquidise, sieve, and bottle when cold.

Pontac Sauce, which sounds as though it ought to come from somewhere in North America, originated in Rutland and Leicestershire, and it is said that it will keep in the bottle for up to seven years. Take two quarts of elderberries stripped from the stalk. Put into a crock or bowl, and pour two quarts of boiling vinegar over them. Stand overnight in an oven set at about 100 degrees centigrade. In the morning strain the liquid into a saucepan, add four blades of mace, a small piece of bruised ginger, a dessertspoon of cloves, two of black peppercorns, and four ounces of chopped shallots. Boil for ten minutes, and pour over the elderberries. Stand for twenty-four hours, put through a liquidiser, sieve and bottle. This is a sharp, spicy sauce that goes very well with steaks, cold meat, and fried fish.

Eschallot Wine is a piquant sauce made from shallots and sherry. Put three ounces of finely chopped shallots into a glass jar and pour in a bottle of dry or medium sherry; close and stand in a sunny window, shaking well every day. After ten days, strain the liquid, and replace the shallots with another three ounces, freshly chopped. Pour back the sherry and repeat the ten-day marination. Strain and bottle. Eschallot Wine goes well with most things, but a good dash added to soup is quite excellent.

VINEGARS AND MUSTARDS

Herb vinegars are excellent in cooking, in particular giving a special difference to a French dressing. The herbs to use are tarragon, lemon balm, basil, chives, burnet, borage leaves, lovage leaves or seeds, dill, celery, caraway, anise, cumin, coriander, primrose flowers, and rose petals. These can be used individually or in combinations, and experiments with other herbs can be both fun and rewarding. Brewing the vinegars is simplicity itself, except for primrose vinegar. All you do is infuse the herbs or flowers in white wine vinegar, in a glass jar standing in a sunny window, for fifteen to twenty days, shaking daily.

Rose Vinegar is made from an ounce of musk rose petals, which have been wilted in the sun for two days (this is not absolutely essential), and infused in a pint of vinegar in a closed jar for fifteen days. The vinegar takes up the scent and colour of the petals, and looks like a fine rosé wine. It is particularly useful with strong, gamey meats, like venison, hare, wild boar or pigeons. The game should be soaked overnight in a marinade of rose petal vinegar, chopped basil, mint, marjoram and the juice of a lemon.

This same method applies to making **Elder Flower** and **Carnation Vinegars**. Elder flower has a very delicate perfume, which is lovely in a salad dressing.

Leafy herbs like basil, mint and salad burnet, can be satisfactorily turned into vinegar in ten days. Seeds take longer, and the best rule of thumb is to double the period of suffusion.

Garlic and shallots make good vinegar, but for something really fiery it is hard to beat **Horseradish Vinegar**. Pour a quart of good vinegar onto three ounces of grated horseradish, an ounce of minced shallots, and one eighth of an ounce of cayenne pepper. Stand for a week. It puts a zest into cold meat.

Primrose Vinegar was a popular Wakefield brew, but does require rather more work than the others. Boil six pounds of coarse brown sugar with four gallons of water for fifteen minutes. After clearing the mixture with the shell and white of an egg, strain the liquid over two gallons of primrose flowers on their stalks. When cold add four ounces of compressed yeast. Stand for two days, stirring regularly. Put into a barrel, and bottle after it turns to vinegar.

Most herb vinegars can be used to make **Mustard**, particularly those flavoured with tarragon, elder, basil, salad burnet, garlic, shallots or celery. Sherry, madeira or champagne can be used. One method is to mix the mustard powder with a vinegar, white wine or water in which grated horseradish has been boiled.

To make a mustard that will keep, pour a quart of boiling herb vinegar, or water, on to two ounces of grated horseradish. Stand for twenty-four hours in a closed container, strain and mix with mustard powder. The texture can be heightened by adding whole mustard seed.

SYRUPS AND CANDIED FLOWERS

Syrups made from herb garden flowers were popular for use with puddings, but more often as a soothing treatment for sore throats, coughs and colds. One of the commonest was **Violet Syrup:** Pour a pint of boiling water over a pound of violets, and cook over a slow heat for two hours. Strain, put the violets in a muslin cloth, and squeeze out the liquid. To every pint of liquid, take two and a half pounds of sugar, and boil it in a quarter of a pint of water until it shows signs of setting, pour in the violet water, cook very slowly until the syrup makes threads. Bottle.

Red field poppies were made into a syrup by the same method, and used to treat colds, while a syrup was made from red cabbage for stomach upsets.

One of the most delightful ways of preserving flowers from the herb garden is to **Candy** them. They are outstandingly attractive decorations for cakes and puddings, or can simply be served as sweets after dinner. Primroses, borage, violet flowers, and rose petals are the best for candying.

Although it is time consuming, candying is simple enough. First make certain that the flower heads are clean and absolutely dry. Whisk up the white of eggs until they are light and bubbly, and with a paintbrush, paint the white onto the flowers, and dip them in caster sugar (some people recommend granulated sugar, but it is rather coarse for this job) making sure that the flower is well coated. Set each one on greaseproof paper spread on a cake rack, and dry in a cool oven, or in the airing cupboard.

Unusual after dinner sweets, which used to be commonly served in the past, are made from candying coriander and caraway seeds by the same method.

WINES AND BEERS

Herbs were widely used to make wines and beers, which were drunk less for their flavour, than for their supposed tonic value. A particularly popular one was **Clover Wine.** Take three quarts of red clover heads, three pounds of sugar, one ounce of yeast, one gallon of water, and the juice of two lemons. Pour two quarts of boiling water over the clover heads, and leave to infuse for twelve hours. Melt half the sugar in a quart of boiling water, and add to the infusion. Put in the yeast and lemon juice. Leave to ferment. After seven days boil the remaining sugar in a quart of water, and add to the fermenting brew. Stand for a day, strain, and let the fermentation work through before bottling.

Daisy Wine is made from two quarts of daisy flower heads to half a gallon of water, two pounds of sugar, the juice of a lemon and orange, and three-quarters of an ounce of yeast.

In the seventeenth century, **Clary Wine**, was greatly valued as an aid to sleep, which is curious since it was also regarded as an aphrodisiac and boost to fertility. To make a large quantity take ten gallons of water, thirteen pounds of sugar, and the well-beaten whites of sixteen eggs. Boil slowly for an hour, skimming all the while, and then leave to get cold. Put a pint of clary flowers, including the stalks and small leaves, into a barrel with a pint of brewers yeast, add the liquid, and stir twice a day until it has stopped working. Seal the barrel, and keep for four months before bottling.

Sage Wine was made as a virtual cure all, but particularly as a defence against the ravages of time and age. Strictly speaking it was less of a home brew than an infusion. Pound up four good handfuls of red sage, put it in a jar and pour in a quart of red wine. Stand for four days, but giving it a good shake each morning. It is then ready for use. A daily dose of three spoonfuls of wine to one of water, followed by an hour's fast, was recommended to be taken from Michaelmas (September 29) to the end of March.

Herb wines can be made successfully from dried herbs, but they must be infused in two quarts of boiling water before the winemaking is begun.

Perhaps the best known of the herb beers is **Nettle Beer**, and the method of brewing can be as well applied to other herbs. Take one gallon of nettles, the tops are best, one and a half pounds of malt, one pound of sugar, two ounces of sarsaparilla, one ounce of hops, one ounce of yeast, and a gallon of water. Boil the nettles and water for half an hour, add the sugar, hops and sarsaparilla. Let the liquid become lukewarm, and add the yeast. Leave it to work.

TEAS

A great many herbs can be made into teas, and it really is a matter of taste which you choose; they can be made with either fresh or dried herbs. Undoubtedly some of them do have a tonic or soothing effect. Comfrey tea tastes like a rather pleasant China tea, and drunk as a nightcap certainly seems to aid sleep.

Horehound Tea needs a bit of titivating to make it palatable, but it does soothe coughs and bronchial troubles. To a good handful of white horehound leaves add boiling water, a tablespoon or two of granulated sugar, and the juice of a lemon.

Oswego Tea, which is made from the beautifully aromatic leaves of bergamot, was devised by the rebellious American colonist after the Boston Tea Party. A few dried flower heads from the herb will give ordinary tea the flavour of a Chinese scented tea.

POT-POURRI

This is one of the most delightful uses of leaves and flowers from the herb garden and borders. Bowls of pot-pourri are not only very attractive scattered around the house, but they also scent the atmosphere in a way that can never be achieved by the horribly artificial smells of an aerosol air-freshener. Pot-pourri is quite simple to make, and can be added to year by year. All that is needed are flower heads and petals, aromatic leaves, and a fixative; the latter can normally be bought from stores that deal in herbs, spices and herbal medicines.

The choice of material for pot-pourri is very considerable; petals of all the sweetly-scented old-fashioned roses, and the leaves of the sweetbriar, carnations and pinks, jasmine, lavender, balm, lemon verbena, bergamot, scented-leaved geraniums, bay leaves, rosemary, violets, mint, thyme, southernwood, lilac, wallflowers, wisteria, lime flowers, costmary, catnip and mint are just a few.

All the flowers should be picked when they are fresh and just opening, and the leaves when they are young, and then dried thoroughly in the airing cupboard. To give the mixture colour – a lot will come from the rose petals – add the dried flowers of blue, carmine and rose cornflowers, marigolds, larkspurs and helichrysums.

The pot-pourri can be added to during the season, as and when flowers and foliage become available. Lay down the dried material and fixative in alternate layers, and stir regularly.

COSMETICS

Herbs have been used for cosmetic purposes from the time of the Ancient Egyptians, and probably the Chinese before them. If you count woad as a cosmetic, and it certainly was used as a body paint, herbal beauty aids were in vogue in very early times in Britain.

An Elizabethan face cream was made from a pound of hog's lard boiled with four ounces of fresh rose petals and four ounces of fresh cowslip leaves for fifteen minutes, strained and set. Fresh elder flowers were used as a substitute for rose petals. Anti-wrinkle mixture was made from buttermilk, camomile, white pond lily leaves, strawberry leaves or elder flowers, and teasel. This was simmered for forty minutes, and left to stand for five hours. It was re-heated and about half an ounce of honey was added. A face pack was made from herbs infused and mixed with Fuller's Earth.

Freckles: Infusion of elder flowers, wood sorrel and daisy heads.

Hair and Scalp Lotion: Infusion of camomile, nettles, parsley and rosemary. Other lotions were made by infusing herbs in alcohol. The most popular for this were thyme, lavender, mint, marjoram, lemon verbena, lemon balm and rosemary.

Hair Rinse: Horsetail and sage infusion.

Hair Colourants: An infusion of mature privet leaves was used to give hair a chestnut hue, and to add a golden gleam to the chestnut, quince juice was included. A rinse made from box leaves is claimed to lighten the hair. Elderberries were used to dye hair black.

BATHS

Soothing baths were made from adding a tablespoon of essential oil of marigold petals and hyssop to the water, or from an infusion of dandelion, horsetail and rosemary. To produce an aromatic bath put dried pennyroyal, sage, rosemary, camomile flower heads, lavender, lemon verbena, lemon balm, angelica and elder flowers into muslin bag. Steep in a quart of boiling water for fifteen minutes before taking the bath, and then put the liquid and the bag into the bath water.

DYES

Herbal or vegetable dyes were for centuries the main source of colour for fabrics and paints. Because they tend not to be fast, they have been largely superseded by chemical dyes. But with the renewed interest in home spinning and weaving, they are making a comeback. A fine range of colours can be obtained from natural sources.

Red: Garden sorrel roots; lady's bedstraw; madder roots.

Blue: Elderberries; chicory leaves; elecampane roots mixed with wood ash and whortleberries; woad leaves; yellow flag flowers.

Yellow: Agrimony; lady's bedstraw stems and leaves; dyer's broom; fumitory flowers; yarrow flowers; toadsflax flowers; St. John's wort flowers.

Green: Elder leaves with alum; hyssop leaves; tansy shoots; lily-of-the-valley leaves; parsley leaves; yarrow leaves.

Purple: Elderberries with alum.

Brown: Hop stalks; teasel flowers; marjoram.

Black: Yellow flag roots; elder roots, and the bark from mature branches.

MEDICINE

Over and above all their other uses, the most important role of herbs throughout history was, and is, in medicine. The very word, drug, comes from the Anglo-Saxon word, drigan, meaning the drying of herbs. Herbs were, and still are, administered in a number of different ways. David Conway, in his book *The Magic of Herbs*, explains just how simple it is to prepare the medicaments.

Infusions: A pint of boiling water poured over an ounce of dried herbs, or three handfuls of fresh herbs. An alternative method is to bring the water and herbs to the boil, and simmer for two minutes. Either way the infusion should be left to brew for about four hours, and then it will stay fresh in a bottle in a cool place for up to four days.

Tisanes: These are brewed like tea for immediate use. One teaspoon of dried or three of fresh herbs for each cup.

Decoctions: Normally these are made from roots. Simmer an ounce of dried root until the liquid has been reduced to half. Store as for an infusion.

Creams and Ointments: Cook an ounce of powdered herbs in three-quarters of a pound of lard until the herbs are completely absorbed into the fat, and strain into a container. The ointment can be hardened by reheating with some beeswax. Fresh and dried herbs can also be thoroughly blended into plain cold cream to make ointments.

Tinctures: Three ounces of powdered herbs to a quart of surgical spirit. Bottle and shake every other day for three weeks before using.

Essential Oils: To extract these put two tablespoonfuls of well crushed and pounded herbs into a half pint bottle, and three-quarters fill with pure vegetable oil, and a tablespoon of plain vinegar. Stand in a window for three weeks, where the mixture will be exposed to as much sunlight as possible. Replace the herbs at the end of the first and second week to increase the strength. In cold, overcast weather the bottle can be plunged in warm water for half an hour, or so, each day.

Poultices: Steep herbs in water until soft, heat the macerated material, and apply to the area to be treated under a tight bandage. Alternatively add an infusion to cornflour to make a thin paste, spread it on a bandage, and apply.

Sleeping Draughts: A good many herbs are credited with aiding sleep, and among the best known infusions are red clover heads, lettuce and hops; mulberry leaves (those from *Morus nigra*), cowslip leaves and mullein; betony leaves; lime leaves.

Tonics: Two classic recipes are infusions of chervil, heather, honeysuckle, red clover and vervain; and lily-of-the-valley, loosestrife, marjoram and vervain.

When seeds are being used in making herbal medicine they should be soaked for twenty-four hours before brewing.

As a general rule dosages are, two or three wine glasses of infusions, and one cupful of decoctions, daily.

6

Where to Grow Herbs
Knots, Mounts and Meadows

Just as the range of herbs, or plants that can be counted as herbs, is enormous, so is the choice of ways in which to grow them. A 'herb garden' can be as simple as a strawberry crock or as complicated as the most intricate knot garden.

The practice of growing herbs in their own special place in gardens goes back a very long way. Merodachbaladan II, who reigned over Babylonia from 721 BC to 710 BC, had a herb garden in which he grew seventy different varieties, and it is clear that herbal medicine must have brought many plants in from the wild. In the seventh century BC an Assyrian record listed nearly one thousand plants used for the treatment of illness and injury. As we have seen, the monks continued this tradition in more recent times, and this seems a good point from which to start looking at ways of cultivating herbs, since their methods were plain and unadorned, and in many ways ideally suited to modern gardens.

Medicinal and culinary herbs were grown in square or oblong beds, quite often raised, intersected by brick, stone or grass paths, and although this might seem somewhat severe, the shape, height, colour and texture of the plants softened the effect. The arrangement and size of the beds made it easy for them to be kept in order, and provided ready access to the plants. A fine example of a monastic physic garden can be seen at Michelham Priory, which is near Hailsham in East Sussex, and it shows how cultivated herbs and Britain's native wild species can be grown side by side.

For the person who has a relatively small garden, and a large enthusiasm for herbs, it is perfectly possible to turn over the entire garden to them, without losing out on the colour and display normally achieved with shrubs, herbaceous borders and beds of annuals because so many of those plants can lay claim to medicinal or culinary connections. Assuming the garden is of a fairly regular shape, it can be divided into a series of beds on the classic herb garden pattern, intersected by paths. Grass will tend to reduce any rigidness that might occur, while, on the other hand, brick or paved paths provide extra growing areas for the prostrate thymes, dwarf mints, pennyroyal and pinks. The paths should all lead to a central point, which, if it is a fairly small area, could be a camomile lawn, or an arbour, or simply a bay tree or juniper.

While the herb collection is planted in the beds, the whole garden can be surrounded by borders of herbaceous flowers, roses, shrubs, bulbs and annuals, backed by herby climbers, such as jasmine, honeysuckle and wisteria. It probably would be rare for anyone to turn the entire garden over to herbs, but more common to give them a place of their own within the complex of the garden. If there is room, a herb garden, perhaps hedged with yew or roses, can be established as a link between the flower and the kitchen garden. Not only does it soften any abrupt transition from the decorative to the utilitarian, but has the practical advantage of having vegetables and herbs in the same area.

A well-tended kitchen garden is, of course, a very attractive part of the garden as a whole. Neatly cultivated rows of crops have a pleasing, almost oriental, austerity, which sets off the colours of the vegetables; shades of green that cover a spectrum from almost daffodil-yellow to blue-grey; reds and purples, blacks and white. To this can be added a herb bed, which will have all the grace and splendour of a fine herbaceous border. Fennel, both green and purple, angelica, with its bold foliage, and magnificent flower and seed heads, towering lovage, the ferny foliage and bright gold flower discs of tansy, silvery-grey wormwood and southernwood, rosemary, bay and juniper, provide the height and background to red and green sage, mauve-flowered thyme, neat bushes of winter savory, feathery caraway and sweet cicily, spreading cushions of gold and green marjoram, blue-green rue, costmary, which has a kind of bloom on its foliage, and mint that comes in so many leaf shapes, shades and textures, and so the list goes on.

Of course it is not necessary to confine herbs to specified plots and beds. They can be allowed to crop up all over the garden. They are a particular asset to a patio, where small beds in the paving can be filled with herbs, such as thyme and sage, and the beautiful prostrate rosemarys. In fact, what could be more convenient than having fresh herbs to hand when cooking a barbecued meal. A moveable patio or terrace herb garden can be formed by growing the plants in different sized terra-cotta pots, arranged like an abstract sculpture. This is an ideal way of cultivating herbs in a tiny town garden, or on a verandah or window sill if you have no garden at all. Many of the smaller varieties, like thyme, marjoram, winter savory, basil, parsley, chervil and chives can be satisfactorily cultivated in a window box, and pots in the kitchen window can be very productive.

Before the landscape movement, one of the glories of medieval and Tudor gardens were the parterres and knots, with their coloured earths and sand, powdered brick dust, and intricate designs in grass, edgings and plants. These days they are regarded as too fussy, and certainly too much work, although there is a renewed interest in formal gardening. The nearest we see to them is the carpet bedding in public recreation areas, which is another reason why they lost favour, since nobody wants to be accused of converting their garden into a municipal park.

Nevertheless, it is possible to borrow the style of knots and parterres, and adapt it to herb growing. The outline of the tapestry-like design can be made with dwarf, clipped box, hyssop, lavender (the compact Hidcote and Munstead varieties, or the pink-flowered, *Rosea*), or even rue, marjoram, winter savory, thyme or sage. When the beds are planted with herbs great care must be taken to use colour to create an embroidered effect. Such a herb garden looks extremely good set in the centre of a formal rose garden.

An alternative is a maze or labyrinth. These do not need to have towering yew hedges, such as you find at Hampton Court and Hever Castle, but can be contrived with the neat, sub-shrubby herbs edging a Gordian Knot of grass paths.

For the gardener who really wants to show off there is the medieval mount. These artificial hills were normally set at one end of the pleasure grounds so that the owner could survey his gardens and estates. Often they were topped with a dining hall, and frequently used as a vantage point from which to shoot driven buck.

In his classic book, *The Formal Garden In England*, Sir Reginald Blomfield describes two medicinal gardens designed by Olivier de Serres, who was gardener to both Louis XIII and Louis XIV, and responsible for laying out part of the gardens at the Louvre, Versailles, Tuileries and St. Germain-en-Laye. His medicinal garden was, in fact, a mount, with a diameter of some two hundred and seventy feet, rising to a height of about fifty feet. Sir Reginald wrote: 'One was to be circular in six stages, ascended by a continuous walk like the Tower of Babel; the other was to be square in six stages, ascended by flights of steps at the four angles. The stages were to be fifteen feet wide – eleven for the path and four for the border of herbs. Each stage was to be six to eight feet high, with retaining walls of masonry, and the interior might be vaulted over as an inner chamber for preserving plants in winter.'

There were much more modest medieval garden ornaments, of which one of the most charming was the turf seat. It is a bench of earth, covered with turf, which can be set against a wall, fence or hedge, under the trees in an orchard, or in an arbour or bower. It is at its most delightful when the seat is planted with camomile or thyme, offering both scent, as well as comfort.

Another pleasing fashion of those days was that of surrounding an orchard with a boundary of borders of sweet herbs. It is the scent of herbs which makes them so important, and a garden is greatly enriched by random groups of the plants, which can be handled where they are to release their wonderful aromas as one walks around.

The increasing interest in our native wild plants, both from the aspect of conservation, and alternative medicine, has brought a new dimension to gardening, particularly the growing of herbs, since nearly all of our endemic species have a herbal use.

Some designers suggest having a wild plant bed in the herb garden, but that can lead to problems. Given the easy life of a well cultivated environment their natural vigour is likely to assert itself, and they could easily revert to being 'noxious weeds'. If there is sufficient available land, the ideal is to create a meadow, undisturbed by plough or spray, and allow the plants to colonise naturally. This process can be aided by the sowing of wild flower seeds, which can now be bought from commercial producers. Under no circumstances should plants be collected from the wild, although there is no harm in gathering seeds of the commoner species. Alternatively, encourage plants to settle in the orchard, or leave a corner of the garden to go native. The spread of seeds can be controlled by cutting before the seeds ripen, leaving just enough to keep up the strength of the colony.

Quite a number of our native plants, such as violets, primroses, wood anemones and wild strawberries, can be cultivated successfully in a horticultural manner. Indeed, some like cowslips and the pasque flower, will, in certain soils, need to have the growing conditions artificially created.

The truly rewarding aspect of growing herbs is that they have something for everyone, and will fit into any garden scheme, from the grandiose to the unadorned.

7
Medicinal Herbs
A Sample of Simples

The shepherds on thy pasture walks
The first fair cowslip finds
Whose tufted flowers on slender stalks
Keep nodding to the winds
And tho thy thorns withold the may
Their shades the violets bring
Which children stoop for in their play
As tokens of the spring
The time when daiseys bloom divine
With thy calm hours begun
And crowflowers blazing blooms are thine
Bright children of the sun
Along thy woodlands shaded nooks
The primrose wanly comes
And shining in thy pebley brooks
The horse bleb gaily blooms

From: April: The Shepherd's Calender by John Clare.

Dr. Samuel Johnson was not a man to get his facts wrong, but he certainly made an error when he described Nicholas Culpeper as 'the man that first ranged the woods and climbed the mountains in search of medicinal and salutary herbs'. Men have been ranging woods, climbing mountains, plunging into deep valleys and ravines, wading through swamps, and tramping open moorland in search of medicinal herbs since just about the beginning of time. Simpling women made their living from gathering wild herbs, and until relatively recent days, countrywomen treated their families with medicines and potions made from the plants they picked in the meadows and hedgerows.

This chapter does not attempt to give a definitive catalogue of British native plants that have a place in the *materia medica*, but to suggest a number that can be grown in the wild garden and the herb beds, that were, and in many cases, still are, treasured for their medicinal qualities. And besides that virtue, they are beautiful in their own right.

ADDER's TONGUE (Ophioglossum vulgatum)

Also known as Adder's Spear, it was used for treating both human and animal ailments. It was prescribed for indigestion, and a green ointment for healing wounds was made by pounding the leaves in a mortar, and boiling the pulp in olive oil. The herb was also regarded as an antidote to snake bite, no doubt because the flower spike was thought to bear a resemblance to an adder's tongue. It was an ingredient in a cattle balm used on wounds, sores, bruises and ulcers.

AGRIMONY (Agrimonia eupatoria)

This is a common meadow and hedgerow plant, easily recognised by its spikes of bright yellow flowers. The Anglo-Saxons used it to cure snake bite, to treat wounds and get rid of warts. It was also employed as a general tonic, and for eye complaints, bad breath, rheumatism, dry coughs, liver upsets, as a febrifuge (a cooling drink), and as a vermifuge (a treatment for worms and other intestinal parasites). In animal husbandry it was used to make a drench, and a linament for massaging horses with tired or strained limbs.

ALDER (Alnus glutinosa)

A sturdy, attractive tree that thrives near water and produces tassles of purple and yellow catkins, it was used to treat kidney complaints, and also to make a balm for sore feet. The veterinary use was for blood ailments, rheumatism and swellings.

ALKANET (Pentaglottis sempervirens)

Originally a garden plant, it long ago escaped into the wild and has established itself in woods and by roadsides, enlivening the countryside with its bright blue flowers. Its varied applications made it particularly valuable. It was used to prepare wool to take deep-coloured dyes. Taken with wine, it was prescribed to relieve kidney pains, and to cure diarrhoea. A linament was prepared from alkanet to treat leprosy, and boiled with wax and oil was an ointment for burns. In the kitchen it was used to colour a medieval dish made from rabbits or kid, known as German Broth.

ANEMONE nemorosa (WOOD ANEMONE) and ANEMONE pulsatilla (PASQUE FLOWER)

The wood anemone is certainly among the loveliest plants. Massed in woodland, it is one of the treasured sights of spring. The pasque flower, now very rare in its natural habitat on chalk downs and hills, is a magnificent garden flower. In fact, both species will do well in cultivation. Medicinally the wood anemone was valued for eye complaints, tooth troubles and ulcers. Eye disorders in animals were treated with the plant, which was also given to them as a tonic. The pasque flower was used for the relief of varicose veins and swollen joints.

ARSMART or WATER PEPPER (Polygonum hydropiper)

A member of the large and handsome polygonum family, this greenish flowered plant thrives in damp and boggy places. In the past the leaves were rubbed into the backs of horses to give them strength, and a handful of the herb was placed under the saddle, in the belief that it would refresh the animal during a long journey.

ASARABACCA (Asarum europaeum)

This plant, with its neat kidney-shaped leaves, and almost tubular purple flowers, could be an escapee into the wild, but whether it is, or is, in fact, a native, it has become rare. Turner called it Azarabacca or Foalfoot, and claimed that it only grew in gardens, which tends to support the notion that it was introduced. It was dried and ground into a snuff to restore the sense of smell, and was taken internally to cure catarrhal deafness. It was also used to treat inflammation of the breast following child-bearing, and for convulsions.

AVENS, WOOD or HERB BENNET (Geum urbanum) and WATER AVENS (Geum rivale)

These are pretty plants with yellow flowers in the case of wood avens, and red in that of water avens, with attractive heads of seeds armed with hooks. In fact it was not the flowers, seeds or leaves that were put to use, but the roots, which were laid among clothes and linen to discourage moths. The whole plant was used to treat animals with heart complaints, digestive problems, vomiting and jaundice.

BARBERRY (Berberis vulgaris)

With its tassels of yellow flowers and bright red berries, this attractive shrub can still be found growing wild, but plants can be bought from good nursery gardens. Both the bark and the berries were used to treat jaundice, and liver and spleen complaints. The berries can be made into a delicious, sharp conserve that makes an excellent relish to be eaten with cold meat.

BETONY (Betonica officinalis)

A common, pink-flowered hedgerow plant, with somewhat nettle-like leaves, it has long been valued for its medicinal properties, particularly as a pain killer. The flowers were made into a conserve and eaten to ease headaches, and a snuff was manufactured for nervous headaches. The herb was also used for neuralgia, epilepsy and nervous disorders in general. Mixed with cumin seed in water it was supposed to prevent vomiting, and the leaves, either chewed or made into a broth were taken for shortness of breath. It was also dried to produce a herbal tobacco. An infusion was used as an eye wash, and there was a belief that if fresh leaves were eaten before a drinking bout, they would stave off drunkenness. The plant was also supposed to prevent nightmares. And, as if that were not enough, betony was prescribed for animals suffering from debility, gastritis, rheumatism, arthritis, sciatica, rickets, boils, abcesses, corns, warts and blisters.

BIRCH (Betula pendula)

The silver birch is one of the most graceful trees, rightly known as the lady of the woods. An infusion of leaves is used for skin complaints, including acne. The essential oils relieve rheumatic pains. A beer is brewed from the sap.

BIRD'S-FOOT TREFOIL or LADIES SLIPPER (Lotus corniculatus)

A bright, cheerful flower that is to be seen growing everywhere, its yellow pea-flowers often boldly splashed with red or orange. It was considered useful for making a gargle, and for keeping the mouth fresh and healthy.

BISTORT (Polygonum bistorta)

Also known as snakeweed, this meadow plant was made into a decoction to soothe sore throats, either as a gargle or a draught. It was also believed to be able to heal internal ulcers.

BLACKBERRY (Rubus fruticosus)

Apart from the common bramble, there are a considerable number of species of blackberries producing edible fruits, all of which are said to be good for people suffering from anaemia. A decoction was made from the roots for children suffering from diarrhoea, and an infusion of the leaves was given as a tonic.

BLUEBELL (Endymion non-scriptus)

A beautiful flower that needs no description. The name alone creates a vision of blue carpeting a wood, and a wonderful, heady scent drawn from the bells by the May sunshine. Despite its loveliness, its uses were strictly utilitarian. Its sticky sap was used as a glue in bookbinding, and even to secure arrow flights. It was also employed in the manufacture of starch. In the past it was known as Crowtoes; Crawtees in the north.

BROOM (Sarothamnus scorparius)

This shrub, with its gleaming yellow flowers, some stained with red, is one of the magical herbs; a fairy plant. At a more mundane level, as a mild diuretic it induces urine, and was also given to people suffering from dropsy and ague. In Master Fitzherbert's *Book of Husbandry*, published in 1534, broom was recommended as a salve for sheep, used as a dip after shearing. He said that a large quantity of the twigs, flowers, leaves, and seed pods should be chopped very fine and boiled in twenty gallons of water until it starts to thicken into a jelly. This was mixed with two pounds of melted sheep's suet, a bottle of old urine, and salt brine and stirred and strained through a cloth. The mixture was stored in containers and made lukewarm before being sponged on to the sheep to heal scab and kill lice. He added that it could be used as a dip before shearing without harming the fleece.

BUGLE (Ajuga reptans)
With its fine blue flowers, and shiny green leaves, it makes excellent ground-cover in a damp, shady place. It was taken as a mild narcotic, and considered an excellent digestive. The infusion was made palatable by the addition of honey. It was also used to treat wounds and ruptures.

BUGLOSS (Echium vulgare)
Another handsome blue-flowered plant, which is found on chalkland. In the sixteenth century it was known as Orchanet, and the roots were made into a red dye used in confectionery, and also as rouge. Medicinally it was made into a draught for chest complaints.

BLACK BRYONY (Tamus communis)
This attractive plant, which is also known as Wild Nep, is one of the truly ancient herbs. The fresh tubers were made into a plaster or ointment for bruises and black eyes, and as a tincture, it was said to be a cure for chilblains. It was also used in the treatment of epilepsy and paralysis, and the young shoots were boiled and eaten to deal with urinary problems. The leaves, pounded with wine, were used as an ointment for sores on animals.

WHITE BRYONY (Bryonia dioica)
In homeopathic medicine this plant is administered for arthritis and

rheumatism. It was also prescribed for a large range of complaints from gout, hysteria, epilepsy and insanity, to deafness. Young shoots were boiled and given for urinary and stomach disorders, while the leaves and red fruits were ground up with salt and applied to ulcers. A decoction made from the roots was a popular skin cleanser, and the juice of the plant was used as a decongestant. Mixed with honey, white bryony was taken for breathlessness, ruptures and convulsions.

BURDOCK (Arctium pubens)

There was a time when the roots of this common plant of woods and wasteland were eaten as a vegetable. Medicinally it was brewed in to what was regarded as a restorative cordial for people recovering from an illness. Anyone trying this should take it with caution, since it is a diuretic. It was used to treat arthritis and rheumatism, and the seeds were made into a medicine for sciatica. A lotion made from the plant was used for skin and scalp problems, and was once used on lepers. Burdock was used on animals for blood disorders, coughs, rheumatism and skin parasites.

LESSER BURDOCK (Arctium minus)

It used to be added to salads because it was believed to have the ability to make people cheerful. It was also put into wine to improve the flavour.

BUTTERCUP (Ranunculus acris)

Not the most popular plant in the garden, because of its invasive habit, nevertheless, it is one of the most strikingly pretty wild flowers, particularly massed in a meadow. It is still used to treat shingles and skin complaints, but must be administered by a qualified herbalist.

CAPER SPURGE (Euphorbia lathyrus)

Regarded now more as a weed, it was valued for its large seed pods, which were pickled and used in sauces. Medicinally it was employed to treat the eye disease, oedema, and for various aches and pains.

GREATER CELANDINE (Chelidonium majus)

This good looking, but invasive plant, once known as Seledine, has always been linked with swallows, because, in ancient times, it was believed that the parent birds used the herb to restore sight to blind chicks, and Pliny the Elder observed that the greater celandine begins flowering when the migratory swallows arrived in the spring, and does not fade until they leave in the early autumn. The plant was used on cataracts, and to stop eyes from watering. The distinctive orange sap was a treatment for rheumatism and head wounds, and to remove warts and corns. It was also used for eye ailments and warts in animals. Since the plant is toxic, one application seems to have been pretty hazardous, and that was using the juice to loosen teeth before extractions. There is a story that Queen Elizabeth I refused to have a tooth pulled, although it was causing her great pain. Her doctors told her to pack the rotten cavity with greater celandine, and pull it herself, which she did. Dioscorides claimed that if the juice was mixed with honey and boiled in a brass vessel, the resulting lotion would sharpen the eyesight.

LESSER CELANDINE (Ranunculus ficaria)

Pansies, lilies, kingcups, daisies,
Let them live upon their praises;
Long as there's a sun that sets
Primroses will have their glory;
Long as there are violets,
They will have a place in story:
There's a flower that shall be mine,
'Tis the little celandine.

Ere a leaf is on a bush,
In the time before the thrush
Has a thought about its nest,
Thou wilt come with half a call,
Spreading out thy glossy breast
Like a careless prodigal;
Telling tales about the sun,
When we've little warmth, or none.

Prophet of delight and mirth,
Scorned and slighted upon earth!
Herald of a mighty band,
Of joyous train ensuing,

55

Singing at my heart's command,
In the lanes my thoughts pursuing,
I will sing, as doth behove,
Hymns in praise of what I love!

From: 'To The Small Celandine' William Wordsworth.

Known as Pilewort and Fygwurt, it was a standard treatment for haemorrhoids, and disorders affecting the veins in general. The juice was mixed with honey for nasal complaints, and with honey and hog's fat for the King's Evil.

CENTAURY (Centaurium erythraea)

This pretty pink-flowered plant of grassland and dunes was used to produce an antiseptic to clean cuts, grazes and scratches. It also made a mouth wash, and a liver tonic. Animals were dosed with centaury when suffering from indigestion, jaundice, liver fluke, wounds, and sore mouths. It was also regarded as a vermifuge.

CHICKWEED (Stellaria media)

More often cursed than welcomed, this common garden weed was once a popular salad vegetable, and was also regarded as a cure for rheumatism, stomach ulcers and internal inflammation. A cool poultice was applied to sore eyes. It was given to animals for digestive problems, diarrhoea, ulcers and rheumatism.

CINQUEFOIL (Potentilla reptans)

There are a large number of native cinquefoils, but the creeping cinquefoil is the one most likely to have been collected by the old herbalists, who knew it as Cynkfoly or Five-Fingered Grass. They valued it as a powerful sedative and pain-killer; as a gargle for swollen tonsils and sore throats, and as a sovereign cure for fever, particularly quotidian fever, when the leaves were mixed with hydromel, or diluted wine and pepper.

The juice was used for liver and lung complaints, poisoning and dysentery. Skin, finger and nail infections were treated with the herb, and the roots were boiled until the liquid reduced to a third, and this was used for the relief of toothache. Rendered into a liquid, it was poured on the hands, according to Dioscorides, as a protection against 'fears and enchantments, therefore take ye the herb when ye moon increaseth, ye sun rising'.

CLEAVERS or GOOSE GRASS (Galium aparine)

A very common plant which will grow anywhere it can take root. Chaplets or garlands were worn to cure a headache. It was also used for urinary troubles, arthritis, fever and jaundice. As a poultice it was applied to cysts, boils and swellings, and it was made into a lotion to cure dandruff. Whole plants were dug up with a wooden spade and fed to sick pigs in their swill, or in wine or milk. It was also used to treat animals with eczema, abscesses, tumours and cancerous growths.

RED CLOVER (Trifolium pratense)

A syrup made from the flowers was a popular medicine for whooping cough, and the flowers were also believed to be a cure for cancer. In addition it was used to treat headaches, neuralgia, nausea, gastric trouble, ulcers and glandular problems. For animals it was regarded in the past, as now, as a tonic for general debility.

CLUBMOSS (Huperzia selago)

This clubmoss, also known as Fir Clubmoss, is pretty common, and the one most likely to have been collected for its medicinal properties. It contains sulphur, and was used as a tonic when it was believed that a blood disorder was affecting the eyes.

COLTSFOOT (Tussilago farfara)

Known as Foalsfoot, and Coughwort, it has always been important in the treatment of respiratory problems, especially bronchitis. The roots were soaked in wine and chewed to ease coughs and throat infections, and the leaves were dried and smoked to relieve persistent coughs. It was recommended that between each puff, the patient should take a sip of sweet wine. The herb is an effective expectorant. Bruised leaves were laid on inflammations, and they were also boiled in hydromel and drunk to expel dead embryos. Animals suffering from coughs, pneumonia, pleurisy, and asthma were treated with coltsfoot, and poultices were made from the herb for abscesses, ulcers, earache and toothache.

COMMON THISTLE (Cirsium vulgare)

This all too familiar plant still has a reputation for producing a useful tonic for the blood and liver. It is made by infusing one and a half ounces of chopped leaves and stalks in a pint of water. Take a wineglass a day.

CORNFLOWER (Centaurea cyanus)

This old and much loved favourite deserves a place in every garden. It is exceptionally rare to see it growing wild in cornfields, but that was where it was collected to be given to patients who had suffered a stroke to ease the resulting paralysis. It was also used as a calmative, and for eye ailments. With animals it was administered for nervous ailments, eye problems, insect bites and wounds.

COUCH GRASS (Agropyron repens)

This scourge of the gardener has gathered a remarkable array of names: squitch, twitch, quitch, quick, quicken, kwigga, wick, wicken, kett, yawl, cassocks, skally, scoil, scutch, stroil, twike, lonachies, rack, sheep's cheese, wizzard, dent-de-chien or dog's-grass. The pounded rhizomes were used to treat wounds, toothache, watery eyes, jaundice and bladder and kidney disorders. It was also regarded as a laxative. Couch grass is one of the herbs used instinctively by animals. Cats and dogs chew it to make them vomit if they are off-colour. Horse breeders considered it to be the best grazing, and dairymen claimed that it produced the sweetest milk. It was also used for constipation, worms, and kidney and bladder problems in animals.

COWSLIP (Primula veris)

I hear it said yon land is poor,
In spite of those rich cowslips there –
And all the singing larks it shoots
To heaven from the cowslips' roots.

From: 'Cowslips and Larks', W. H. Davies.

This beautiful, sweetly scented flower is now protected, and should never be removed from the wild. However, seed can be bought from seedsmen dealing in native wild flowers, and the plant is a delightful addition to any garden. Like so many popular flowers it has gained different local names over the centuries, such as Pagle, Cowslap, Palsywort and Our-Lady's-Bunch-of-Keys. Regarded as a mild narcotic, it was used to ease pain and aid sleep, and was normally administered as a tea or made into a wine. As one of its names suggests, it was used to treat various degrees of paralysis. It was also administered to relieve pains in the joints, for vertigo and buzzing in the ears. Stockmen and grooms used cowslip to quieten nervous and excitable animals. Cosmetically the flowers were made into a cream for removing wrinkles and improving the skin.

The leaves were used in salads, and in the eighteenth century **Cowslip Pudding** was a favourite dish. To make it you needed a peck of flowers, pounded and chopped, half a pound of grated biscuit, and three pints of cream. Boil the mixture for a short time, and take off the heat. Beat up sixteen eggs with a little cream and rose water, sweeten, and mix all the ingredients together. Pour into a buttered dish and bake. Dust with sugar and serve.

DAISY (Bellis perennis)

The daisy is a very good reason for not using a selective weedkiller on the lawn. No doubt to the horror of lawn fanciers, I can think of few more agreeable sights than a lawn starred with daisies. An infusion of the leaves was thought good for the circulation and those who suffer from chilblains. The plant is also made into a lotion for the complexion, especially when treating acne and boils. An ointment made from the pounded leaves was applied to take the soreness out of bruises. The plant also formed the base of a medicine for catarrh, and varicose veins. Farmers made up a daisy mixture for animals with skin complaints and bruises.

DANDELIONS (Taraxacum offinale)

This is certainly one plant that is known to everyone, whether they live in the country or the town, and has historically been regarded as a health-giving herb. At one time Dandelion Stout was sold as a tonic, especially recommended for the kidneys and liver, circulatory problems, and arthritis. The thick milky juice was used to clear spots and pimples. The roasted roots are ground to powder and added to coffee, and the whole plant is supposed to restore a lost appetite. In animal care dandelion is fed to correct skin and liver disorders, and constipation. A **Dandelion Sandwich** is an unusual and pleasant addition to a picnic or tea in the garden. Butter a slice of white bread and sprinkle with Worcestershire Sauce, cover with a thick layer of finely chopped dandelion leaves, and close with a slice of buttered brown bread.

DANEWORT (Sambucus ebulis)

Legend has it that this low-growing elderberry sprang from the spot on which a Dane fell in battle. It has more pink in the blossom than our familiar roadside tree, and some writers claim that it is poisonous, although that seems inconsistent with it being given the designation, wort, which always indicates a medicinal herb. The leaves, according to Pliny the Elder, were used to soothe and heal burns and scalds, and mixed with barley groats, were laid on the bites of mad dogs. They were also used for impostumes of the brain. Apart from being made into a black hair dye, the berries were a treatment for gout, urinary complaints, and used to kill fleas. Animals were given danewort for dropsy, and inflammation of the uterus and vagina.

DITTANDER (Lepidium latifolium)

Also known as Dittany, Pepperwurt, or Poor Man's Pepper, this is no longer a very common plant, but at one time the fiery tasting roots were ground up and used as a pepper substitute. The roots were also made into a plaster and applied to the buttocks to ease the pain of sciatica.

BROAD LEAVED DOCK (Rumex obtusifolia)

There are a large number of dock species, but the broad leaved dock is probably the most familiar. Its name derives from the Saxon, Docca, and appears in other forms such as Doccan, Doken and Dokken. Every country child knows that the leaves soothe nettle stings. They are also a dressing for blisters on the feet. The plant was used to treat animals for skin inflammation, fever, piles and wounds.

DODDER (Cuscuta europaea)

A parasitic plant, also known as Our Lady's Laces. It was eaten as a pot-herb, served like asparagus. Cooks added it to peas and beans in the belief that it made them cook faster.

ELDER (Sambucus nigra)

There can hardly be a hedgerow or ditch, wood or wasteland in England and Wales where this small tree has not got a good roothold. Usually it is ruthlessly destroyed in gardens, despite the fact that its distinctive foliage, large umbels of creamy-white flowers and clusters of purple-blue fruits are extremely attractive. It has been used in medicine, cosmetics, cookery, brewing and farming for centuries. In the past it was known as the Boure Tree, and was believed to have provided the wood for the cross upon which Christ was crucified. It was also said to be the tree from which Judas hanged himself. The leaves infused with honey were used for skin complaints, while an infusion of the flowers was drunk by people suffering from catarrh, coughs and colds. The berries were taken as a mild laxative. Elder-based medicines were given for fevers and blood disorders, and the herb was made up into lotions for soothing the pain of burns and scalds. A gargle was made from elder flowers, a large pinch of sage, a teaspoonful of honey, and one of lemon juice or vinegar. It is one of the most versatile of plants. The flowers make a delicious, delicately scented vinegar. Both the flowers and berries are made into wine, while the berries on their own lend a distinctive tang to pies and jellies.

An unusual and delightful pudding is **Elder Flower Fritters**. Well washed heads of freshly picked flowers are dipped in a pancake batter and fried. The fritters should be powdered with sugar and served with a wedge of fresh lemon. Another method of making fritters is to pound the flowers in a mortar, and mix with cream cheese and grated parmesan, fresh eggs, a little cinnamon, and a few drops of rose water. Beat to a smooth, stiff paste, form into small balls, and fry in butter. Serve with a dusting of sugar.

A curious, and once popular pudding, is **Elder Milk**. To make it pick two good clusters of flowers, and strip them from the stalks. Simmer for ten minutes in a quart of milk. Add a spoonful of semolina, and whisk together with sugar, a pinch of salt, and two egg yolks. Pour into a bowl and decorate with white of egg beaten with sugar. Sprinkle with sugar and cinnamon, and serve.

A favourite eighteenth-century bedtime drink was mulled elderberry wine, with nutmeg and small pieces of toast. Its popularity probably had something to do with the conviction that the berries were an aid to longevity. **Spicy Imitation Bamboo Shoots** were made from the largest, and youngest, shoots of elder cut about the middle of May. Peel off the skin and lay the shoots in a strong brine of salt and water for twenty-four hours. Dry them individually. Make a pickle of half of white wine and half of beer. To a quart of the liquid put an ounce of red or white pepper, an ounce of sliced ginger, a little mace, and some pepper corns. Boil and pour the hot liquid over the elderberry. Seal and leave in a warm place for an hour or so.

Another unusual relish is **Elderberry Chutney**. Pick and weigh two pounds of elderberries, wash well and crush in a saucepan with a wooden spoon or pestle. Finely chop a large onion. Add it, and a pint of vinegar, a teaspoon of salt, a teaspoon of ground ginger, half a teaspoon of cayenne pepper and mixed spices, and a teaspoon of mustard seed. Bring to the boil and simmer until the mixture thickens. Put in jars and cover.

Like the fruits of the Danewort, elderberries were used to dye hair black, and the flowers and fruit were used to make cosmetic washes to soften the skin and tone up the muscles. A balm made from the flowers was used to reduce crow's feet around the eyes. For centuries the hollowed stems of the twigs and branches have been used by children to make peashooters, whistles and flutes. Farmers used to whip corn, fruit trees and vegetables with the green leaves to keep off blight.

EYEBRIGHT (Euphrasia nemorosa)

A fairly insignificant looking plant, which, as its name suggests, was used to improve eyesight. The Greeks named it after the linnet, because in legend the little songbird was said to have discovered its healing powers. Its reputation for curing failing sight was widespread throughout Europe. In France its name is Casselunettes, a reference to the fact that spectacles are not needed after using it. The Italians have given it the lovely name, Luminella, light for the eyes. Its botanical name is taken from Euphrosyne, one of the Graces. It was used for measles in an attempt to prevent eye damage, and for treating conjunctivitis, and weak and inflamed eyes in animals. An eye lotion was made from the whole plant mixed with rose water, and a tincture produced from eyebright was mixed with slightly salted water before use. Spleen, stomach and gall-bladder complaints, and indigestion were treated with an infusion of the herb.

FENUGREEK (Trifolium ornithopodioides)

An ancient herb, it was used to treat a wide variety of female disorders. Mixed with cress seeds and vinegar it was given to lepers, and was also used for stomach ulcers, gout, gangrene, and persistent coughs. A decoction was supposed to be an effective underarm deodorant, and it was also employed as a skin cleanser, and to get rid of pimples, freckles, scurf and dandruff. For animals it was prescribed for gastric problems, and made into a poultice for boils, abscesses and sores.

FIGWORT (Scrophularia nodosa)

A tall, robust plant, with attractive small purple and yellow flowers, it was made into an infusion for sore throats and tonsils, high blood pressure, circulatory disorders, and varicose veins. It is a diuretic.

FUMITORY (Fumaria officinalis)

This familiar purple-flowered plant could, at first glance be mistaken for a vetch. It is said to have got its name from being burned to produce an incense for sorcery. Country girls used it to make a face wash to give them a fair complexion, and it was certainly used for skin complaints, and to get rid of freckles. As a medicine it was used to shift obstructions in the viscera, and especially the liver; for bilious attacks, nausea, vomiting and stomach cramps. It was also regarded as a useful tonic. The infusion was normally made with wine, although water will do. Dried leaves were smoked as a treatment for head complaints, and it was used on animals for skin complaints, eczema, wounds and liver ailments.

GROUND IVY (Glechoma hederacea)

This pungent, familiar ground coverer, has a number of local names, such as Gill-o'-the-Ground, Maids-in-the-Hay, Hay-Maids, Sat's-Foot, Ale-Hoof, Tun-Hoof, Hove, and Wallwort. As at least two of its names suggest, at one time it was used in brewing beer. Its strong smell was said to drive off serpents, and it was tied around the neck as a defence against scorpions. Its medicinal uses included a treatment for headaches, liver and lung complaints, deafness and healing fresh wounds. As a potent decongestant, it was given as a relief for coughs and colds, and also as an aid to digestion. It was made into a tisane, and drunk as a tonic. Combined with celandine, daisies, rose water and a little sugar, it was used as eyedrops, being dripped into the eyes with a feather. With animals it was used for coughs, ulcers and boils.

GROUNDSEL (Senecio vulgaris)

Another very common garden weed, it too has collected many names; Grundswel, Groundeswele, Grundy-Swallow, Swally, Grinning-Swallow, and Grunsell, among others. It was believed that if someone was suffering from toothache they should draw a circle round the plant with an iron instrument, dig it up, touch the offending tooth with it three times, spitting each time, replant the herb, and thenceforth the tooth would never ache again. There are mixed views about groundsel. Some herbal doctors claim that it has no medicinal use whatsoever, while others recommend it for sinews, sciatica, jaundice, bladder, heart and liver. People suffering from heart disease were advised to eat it in a salad with ordinary meals, and it is true that it was a popular salad herb for a very long time. Dioscorides said that it should be mixed with wine to soothe inflammation of the genitals and anus. Farmers used it to deal with eye complaints and debility in their stock.

HART'S TONGUE (Asplenium scolopendrium)

A very familiar and attractive fern that thrives in damp shady nooks in the garden. The leaves were boiled in red wine, and used to treat upset stomachs and snake bite. For animals it was used to dose colic, dysentery, diarrhoea, and wounds.

HAWKWEED (Pilosella officinarum)

Also known as Mouse-ear, its first name reaches back to the ancient Greek belief that hawks browsed on the plant to give them keen eyesight. A lotion was made of the herb with milk for eye complaints, and it was drunk as a tisane to strengthen the eyes. A decoction of the juice was used to temper steel, and it was claimed that steel-edged tools treated thus could cut stone or iron without being blunted.

HEARTSEASE (Viola arvensis) and (Viola tricolor)

The wild pansies are among the most charming of our native plants, and as a consequence have attracted a number of different names, such as: Knapweed, Bullweed, Matsillon, Herb Trinity, Pansies, Love-in-Idle-ness, Cull-me-to-You, and Three-Faces-in-a-Hood. Medicinally it was used to treat valvular disorders of the heart, asthma, catarrh and epilepsy. A lotion was made for sores and skin ailments.

HEATHER (Erica cinerea)

A widespread plant of moorland and dry heaths, it makes a pleasant garden plant. An infusion was a popular tonic taken after a debilitating illness.

HEMLOCK (Conium maculatum)

This common weed has a deservedly sinister reputation. It is extremely poisonous, and in ancient Greece was used as a method of execution. Socrates ended his life by swallowing a hemlock drink. Medicinally it was used to treat eye, nose and ear disorders. An unpleasant, and doubtless dangerous, practice was to smear hemlock on the breasts of young virgins in the belief that the herb would inhibit their development. The same treatment was applied to the testicles of young boys to prevent thoughts of illicit sex.

HENBANE (Hyoscyamus niger)

With its pale leaves and purple-stained flowers, it really does look like a witch's plant, and it is poisonous, particularly, as its name suggests, to poultry. It was believed that if you bathed your feet in a decoction of henbane, this would induce sleep, and a large pinch of the dried herb was put into the bath to achieve the same effect. The leaves were used to line shoes to prevent tired feet. The herb was also used as a painkiller, and for coughs and catarrh. It was curious that it was used as a medicine for the insane, since it was said that if a person ate a plateful of the boiled leaves their mind would become deranged. Certainly not an experiment to try.

HERB PARIS (Paris quadrifolia)

This interesting and rather rare plant should be grown as a curiosity, than for any practical use, as it is dangerous. It was used for eyes, cramps, convulsions and asthma.

HERB ROBERT (Geranium robertianum)

Also known as Stinking Robert because of the powerful, rank odour emitted from the crushed foliage. It was used to treat ulcers, tumours and wounds in humans, and haemorrhages, kidney and bladder complaints in animals.

HONEYSUCKLE (Lonicera periclymenum)

This glorious climber has a scent which is the essence of the English summer. It was valued for treating head complaints, colds, coughs, sore throats, asthma, rheumatism, arthritis, dropsy, liver and skin complaints. **Syrup of Honeysuckle** is supposed to ensure longevity. To make it gather four pounds of fresh petals, pour eight pints of boiling water over them, and stand for twelve hours in a covered container. Add white sugar to twice the weight of the petals and make into a syrup. In treating animals the herb was used for heart problems, asthma, coughs, rheumatism, worms and skin complaints.

HORSE TAIL OR MARE'S TAIL (Equisetum arvense)

A pernicious plant in the garden, although it does have an undoubted primeval beauty. It can be kept under control in an odd corner. The leaves were used in an infusion to check haemorrhages, diarrhoea and excessive body fluid. An infusion made from the chopped stem was used as a liver and kidney tonic. It was also valued for internal and external ulcers. Put into a bath it was said to ease pain, and it was used in the form of a lotion for shingles and wounds. In boiling water it produced an inhalant for congestion of the chest and nasal passages. The herb was also prescribed for styes, and tenderness and swellings of the eyes. The essential oil was nightly rubbed on to brittle fingernails. Horsetail was used for healing wounded animals.

IVY (Hedera helix)

Far too familiar to need description, ivy does not feature very largely in the *materia medica*, although at one time five berries were crushed and mixed with oil of roses, and after being heated in a pomegranate skin, the brew was dropped in the ears to cure toothache.

KNAPWEED (Centaurea nigra)

Also known as Hardheads, this is a handsome plant with purple, thistle-like flowers. Unmarried country girls used to keep a bunch of knapweed under their bodices in the belief that it would flower when they met their future husbands. Medicinally it was used for glandular ailments, and was mixed with speedwell to relieve catarrh. It was also given to patients recovering from an illness to stimulate their appetite. Gastritis, bruises, sores, and loss of appetite in animals were treated with the herb.

LADY'S SLIPPER (Cypripedium calceolus)

The largest and loveliest of our native orchids, it is now extremely rare in the wild, and should never be collected. Fortunately it is readily available commercially, and makes a superb garden plant, given plenty of protection from slugs and snails. The root was used in an eye ointment.

LADY'S SMOCK (Cardamine pratensis)

One of the Marion flowers, it is also among the prettiest to be found in the fields and hedgerows. Also known as cuckoo flower, the young leaves were eaten in salads, and greatly valued as an anti-scorbutic, and for skin and liver disorders. Young animals suffering from nervous illnesses and convulsions were treated with the herb.

YELLOW LOOSESTRIFE (Lysimachia vulgaris) and PURPLE LOOSESTRIFE (Lythrum salicaria)

While they are not botanically related, both these attractive plants were used to treat eye diseases, usually in the form of a lotion.

MADDER (Rubia peregrina)

A climbing weed, normally found growing quite close to the coast, it was used for dying wool and leather. Medicinally it was used for urinary problems and as a blood purifier.

MAIDENHAIR FERN (Adiantum capillus-veneris)

A delicate and most attractive plant, it was eaten raw, or taken in an infusion, for heart and lung problems. As a lotion it was used to inhibit baldness.

MEADOW CROWFOOT (Ranunculus scelleratus)

A member of the buttercup family, its small yellow flowers are considerably less flamboyant than its larger meadow cousin. It was used to relieve the discomfort of inflamed eyes.

MEADOW SWEET (Filipendula ulmeria)

One of the true beauties of the meadows, ditches, and the banks of rivers and streams. Both the leaves and flowers were used as strewing herbs, and they were added to beer and other drinks for their fragrance. A distilled water made from the flowers was used as drops for the relief of sore and itching eyes. The herb was also used for the treatment of skin complaints, rheumatism and upset stomachs. Farmers gave it to their animals suffering from diarrhoea, fever, and blood disorders. **Meadow Sweet Beer** was a popular tonic. Using dried herbs, mix equal quantities of Meadow Sweet, Dandelion and Agrimony, and add at the rate of two ounces to every gallon of water. Boil for twenty minutes. Strain and add half a pint of yeast and two pounds of sugar. Stand in a warm place for twelve hours, and then bottle.

MELILOT (Melilotus officinalis)

Its yellow, pea-like flowers are loved by bees, and both the flowers and seeds are used to flavour Gruyere cheese. The Chinese eat it to make their bodies smell sweet; a kind of overall deodorant. A tisane was drunk to cure flatulence. Its veterinary use was for colic, stomach upsets, poultices for bruises, skin diseases and eye complaints.

MUGWORT (Artemesia vulgaris)

A prolific plant, it has pleasing grey-green foliage, and an aromatic scent. It was used in baths to relieve fatigue, and pilgrims and wayfarers packed it in their shoes to avoid sore feet. One of the many treatments for the King's Evil made use of the herb. One of the 'good' plants, it was hung over house doors on Midsummer Day to ward off evil spirits, and it was believed that it would prevent ghosts from haunting.

MULLEIN (Verbascum thapsis)

A tall, striking plant, it has soft furry, silver-grey foliage, and candle-spikes of beautiful daffodil-yellow flowers. Its popularity has earned it many different names, such as High-tapers, Long-torch, Felt-wyrt, Softie, Blanket-leaf, Adam's Flannel, Velvet-leaf, Mullen Higgis, Taper and Longe Wurt. The leaves were boiled in milk to produce a medicine for coughs and asthma, and were made into a cough syrup with honey. As its old name Longe Wurt suggests, it was valued for treating all chest complaints, as well as making up into a gargle for sore throats and tonsillitis, and a linctus for deafness caused by catarrh. It was also used as a pain killer and sedative, and as an antidote to scorpion stings.

In very ancient times the woolly leaves were twisted into wicks for lamps. Figs were wrapped in the leaves to keep them fresh, and the flowers were made into a rinse to bring out the highlights in the hair. Mullein was also used to dose animals suffering from coughs, pneumonia, pleurisy, bronchitis, tuberculosis, asthma and diarrhoea, and for making poultices for neuralgic pains and cramps.

NETTLE (Urtica dioica)

One of the most versatile and successful of the wild herbs, nettles have a capacity to survive and flourish under almost any conditions. During the Second World War they were recommended as a nutritious vegetable. It is regarded as being especially effective in treating rheumatism and poor circulation, and stoic sufferers are advised to roll naked in a nettlebed as part of their treatment. It is claimed as a cure for bronchitis, and was used to lessen the risk of haemorrhages, while a decoction of the roots was used for kidney complaints. There was a time when nettles were rubbed all over the bodies of people in comas in an attempt to rouse them, and the herb was mixed with fat as an ointment for external ulcers.

Dog bites, gout, nettle rash, asthma and burns all got the nettle treatment. Made into a drink with salt and hydromel, it was said to expel worms, while the seeds mixed with honey and water were swallowed to induce vomiting after a meal. Boiled with mussels it was used to cure constipation, and in the form of a liniment, was valued as a hair restorative. Green nettles are an enriching addition to compost, and poultrymen used to fatten their birds on the plant, which was fed dried to cattle and horses as a tonic and worm preventative. Animals suffering from rheumatism, paralysis and arthritis were given the herb. The tops of nettles were used in sixteenth century salads, and indeed only the young fresh growth should be used in cooking.

There is an interesting **Russian Nettle Soup** made with equal quantities of nettles, sorrel and spinach. Thoroughly wash the young leaves and boil in salted water, to which a pinch of soda has been added. When cooked, liquidise and put through a sieve. Melt about two ounces of butter and lightly fry three tablespoonfuls of chopped onion leaves, you can use the leaves of Welsh onions, Egyptian tree onions or chives, mixed with half a tablespoonful of flour. Add the puree and a bouillon made in the usual way, and bring to the boil. Serve with sour cream, and sliced and fried hard-boiled eggs.

DEAD NETTLE (Lamium album)
In no way related to the stinging nettle, this good-looking, if rather pungent plant, was used to treat bruises, severe burns, the King's Evil, gout and shingles.

NIGHTSHADE (Solanum nigra and Solanum dulcamara)
Once commonly known as Pety Morel, the leaves and roots were used to provoke urine, and bring on delayed periods. It was also used to

produce a liniment for impostumes, while the seed was made into a medicine for coughs and respiratory problems. Mixed with wine it was regarded as an antidote to poisonous bites and stings, and was mingled with rue to induce vomiting. Nightshade was also employed in the treatment of ruptures, convulsions, paralysis, hay fever, stomach complaints and earache.

ORPINE (Sedum telephium)

Known as Livelong, Live-for-Ever, and Midsummer Men, this pretty stonecrop used to be grown by cottagers in pots and large sea-shells. Sweethearts were given sprigs to ensure their constancy. Medicinally it was applied to wounds, and made into a medicine for catarrh, but it was more valued as a cosmetic. Either fresh or in powder form it was put on to freckles and facial spots. When it was used to cleanse leprous or scurfy eruptions of the skin, the treated areas were afterwards rubbed with barley meal.

OXEYE (Chrysanthemum leucanthemum)

This superb daisy is often seen in huge flowering masses on railway embankments from June to August. The young shoots were eaten as a vegetable, and it was also made into a salve with wax to remove hard swellings.

PELLITORY OF THE WALL (Parietaria judaica)

As its name implies, it thrives on old walls, and has long been cultivated as a medicinal herb, although at one time the young leaves were eaten in salads. Taken as an infusion or as a syrup, it was a treatment for bladder and kidney diseases. The juice was mixed with white lead to make an ointment for shingles and St. Anthony's Fire. It must have done more harm than good.

PENNYWORT (Umbilicus rupestris)

With its tubular creamy-green flowers, this is a very good plant for walls and rock crevices. Since it affects the heart, this is not a herb to be used by any but experts. It was prescribed for epilepsy, kidney disorders, some eye complaints, and pains in the navel.

SCARLET PIMPERNEL (Anagallis arvensis) and BOG PIMPERNEL (Anagallis tenella)

With its brilliant scarlet flowers, the scarlet pimpernel is one of the brightest of our native plants, and even if it can become a bit of a nuisance in the garden, one can't help but be fond of it. It was widely used in medicine to treat jaundice, dropsy, snake and mad dog bites, to draw splinters and thorns, and as a tonic for depression. In powdered form it was sniffed up the nose to ease toothache. The juice was mixed with honey to treat bruises, and made into a lotion to remove freckles and minor skin blemishes. It was greatly valued for eye complaints, and in ancient times the juice was used to dilate the eyes prior to a cataract operation. With animals it was used for epilepsy, and liver and kidney disorders. A curious ritual was observed whilst gathering the herb. It had to be collected before sunrise, with the collector bidding it 'good morning' three times, before uttering any other words that morning. Then it was dug up and thrown into the air. Only after all this had been carried out could the juice be expressed. Bog pimpernel, with its deep pink flowers, is excellent ground cover in a damp place.

PLANTAIN (Plantago major)

Not a great favourite with gardeners, especially those who cherish their lawns, this persistent weed once occupied an important place in the *materia medica*, when it was also known as Waybread or Great Waybread. It was used to treat bronchitis, asthma, and other respiratory complaints; the King's Evil, indigestion, ulcers, dropsy, earache and bleeding gums. Fresh leaves are soothing to stings and wounds, and the herb was used in place of cauterizing in the case of septic wounds. The seeds served as a substitute for linseed in dealing with gum ulcers, while the root and juice were recommended for the relief of toothache. Upset stomachs were settled by either eating the plant as a vegetable, in a gruel or broth, or as a pottage made with wheat. Love philtres were made from the seed heads, and animals were dosed with plantain for dysentery, haemorrhages, fever, wounds, sores, ulcers and bites.

PLOUGHMAN'S SPIKENARD (Inula coynza)

Although a member of the same species, it should not be confused with

Elecampane. It has much smaller flowers and leaves, both of which were used to treat skin complaints, and pains in the legs, ankles and feet.

COMMON POLYPODY (Polypodium vulgare)
One of the prettiest and neatest of the ferns, it grows on the tops of walls, rocks and the trunks of mature trees. It has long been in use in herbal medicine for doctoring coughs, whooping cough and bile.

RED POPPY (Papaver rhoeas)
This is the familiar poppy of cornfields and Armistice Day, once known as Chesboul, and Red Cornrose, and judging by the discovery of seeds in neolithic sites, it has been used to treat the sick from the earliest times. An infusion of leaves and petals was used to soothe sore throats and chests. It was also prescribed for hay fever, asthma and catarrh. The seed heads were mixed with linseed and olive oil to make poultices for swellings, and aches and pains. Animals were given poppies for pneumonia, asthma and eye ailments.

OPIUM POPPY (Papaver somniferum)
One hesitates to discuss this plant, since its cultivation abroad is the source of heroin, and all the evil and destruction associated with that misused drug. It has escaped into the wild, but was possibly first brought to Britain by the Romans. The leaves were boiled in water and a little sugar to make a sleeping draught, and without sugar the liquid was used to bathe head, temples and feet for the same effect. The seed heads were boiled first in water, and then honey, to produce a cough linctus, while the bruised seeds were used for stomach ills, and to ease pain. Mixed with egg yolk and saffron, the herb made a salve for inflamed eyes. In cooking the seeds are used especially in bread-making. They were also parched and mixed with honey as a sweetmeat. Oil expressed from them is said to keep better than olive oil, and was certainly used in salad dressing in Northern France.

PRIMROSE (Primula vulgaris)
Justly one of the best loved of all our wild flowers, it has long been employed in medicine and cookery. As a mild narcotic, it was taken by

insomniacs. It was also used to treat skin complaints, rheumatism, arthritis, and as a general tonic. Animals suffering from fits, paralysis, rheumatism, sciatica and worms were given the herb. In the past **Primrose Pottage** was given to invalids. To make it, pound or put through a food processor, half a pound of rice flour, two ounces of almonds, half an ounce of honey and saffron, and a good quantity of primrose flowers. Mix with almond milk and ginger, and bring to the boil. Sprinkle with primrose flowers and serve.

PURPLE ORCHID (Orchis mascula)

This prolific and very attractive flower of woodland and natural grassland, was once a popular aphrodisiac, and used in making salep, a drink so celebrated in the eighteenth century that there were salep houses in London. Pliny the Elder gave it the name Satyrion, and waxed enthusiastically about its supposed aphrodisiac qualities, which probably owed more to the Doctrine of Signatures, because the roots were supposed to look like testes, than to any real effect. The roots were made into a drink with ewe's milk to induce tumescence, while the opposite result was supposed to be achieved if the draught was made with water. Some individual plants were reputed to be so powerful that a man only had to hold part of its root in his hand to be seized by an over-powering lust. Theophrastus claimed that after touching the purple orchid a man was able to couple with a woman seventy times. After all that it is scarcely surprising that the plant was used in witchcraft and sorcery. Farmers made it into physic for animals suffering from sterility, abortion, diarrhoea and dysentery.

RAGWORT (Senecio jacobaea)

A common and colourful plant bearing masses of bright yellow flowers, it was used for hayfever, despite the fact that its pollen is one of the causes of the ailment. It was also made into a general tonic, and into a lotion for skin complaints in animals.

RESTHARROW (Onionis repens)

Given the right conditions this purple-flowered plant will form dense mats. A decoction made from it was regarded as a cure for piles, and it was also used for kidney stones, ulcers, and toothache. Animals were given it for loss of hair, and kidney and bladder problems.

DOG ROSE (Rosa canina)

In a wild part of the garden, this lovely rose will develop into a fine shrub. Fresh or dried flowers were infused to produce a medicine for heart and brain diseases, as well as for catarrh, stomach upsets, and gynaecological disorders. The root was claimed as a cure for rabies. The herb was used to treat animals with catarrh, diarrhoea, haemorrhages and eye complaints.

ROYAL FERN (Osmunda regalis)

This striking, statuesque fern deserves a place in every garden. It will survive pretty dry conditions, but prefers to grow close to water. It has had several names; Osmunde, Water Fern, and St. Christopher's Fern. The latter name came from the legend that it originally grew from the staff Christ told St. Christopher to plant in the bank after the saint had carried him across the river. It was put into a broth with other herbs for people who had been wounded, and also used to treat heavy bruising, dislocations and even broken bones.

SAMPHIRE (Crithmum maritimum)

This fleshy plant of coastal flats and salt marshes has long been regarded as a delicacy. The shoots are eaten fresh or pickled. The name is a corruption of St. Pierre, and it is dedicated to St. Peter. It can be grown in the herb garden or border. At one time it was used to clear sticky or gummy eyes, and made into a plaster with fried barley, it was used to bring down swelling of the eyes.

SANICLE (Sanicula europaea)

Apart from treating catarrh and inflammations, the juice was drunk to aid the healing of wounds. An infusion or decoction of the roots was used directly on wounds and swellings, and as a nasal douche.

SCABIOUS (Knautia arvensis)

A lovely plant in or outside the garden, it was once known as Matfellon, and used on animals for skin, heart and venereal diseases.

SEA HOLLY (Eryngium maritimum)

This splendid blue-grey thistle needs really sandy soil if it is to survive away from the coast. Farmers used it to make a medicine for their animals with liver and glandular complaints, chest pains, constipation and nervous disorders.

SEA LAVENDER (Limonium vulgare)

Another plant of salt marshes, it has attractive tufts of lavender-coloured flowers. It was used in a treatment designed to correct squinting.

SHEPHERD'S PURSE (Capsella bursa-pastoris)

Also known as Shepherd's Bag, it is generally regarded as a tiresome garden invader, but it was valued as an aid to stop bleeding, either taken as a decoction, as a poultice, or in a bath. The whole plant was used to make a treatment for rheumatism in the joints, and the juice was expressed to ease earache. Haemorrhages, deep wounds and kidney disease in animals were doctored with the plant.

SKULL-CAP (Scutellaria galericulata)

A most attractive blue-flowered plant that grows well in damp conditions, or beside a pond or stream, it is claimed that it effectively reduces withdrawal symptoms in people trying to give up drug and alcohol addiction. It was also valued for nervous tension, insomnia, epilepsy, convulsions and chorea (St. Vitus's dance), and for hysteria, meningitis and gastro-enteritis in animals.

SOAPWORT (Saponaria officinalis)

An extremely useful plant in the past, it is attractive in the garden. One of its uses was washing wool. Pliny the Elder wrote: '.... the juice whereof Fullers use so much to scoure their wooll withall: and wonderful it is to see how white, how pure, how neat and soft it will make it'. It was put with stewing meat to give it a good colour, while medicinally it was used for coughs, liver complaints, leprosy, to halt sneezing, and improve eyesight.

SOWTHISTLE (Sonchos oleraceus)

It is possible that this all too familiar plant was once eaten as a vegetable by the poor, but whether only the roots or leaves, or the entire plant is not clear. Certainly young tender shoots were put in salads. The juice was used as a skin cleanser and was also said to restore sanity to mad hares. The herb was chewed to sweeten the breath, and was boiled in broth and eaten by wet nurses to ensure a good supply of milk. A treatment for urinary problems and abscesses was made from sowthistle. Its juice mixed with salt and olive oil was supposed to restore hearing, while the juice on its own was swallowed to ease stomach pains. Animals suffering from fever and skin complaints were given the plant.

SPEEDWELL (Veronica officinale)

A lovely bright blue flower, the whole flowering plant was used for catarrh, bronchitis, asthma and digestive difficulties. Either as a lotion or a medicine it was a treatment for sores, ulcers, pimples, eczema and pruritis. The herb was used on animals for coughs, bronchial asthma, catarrh and eczema.

SPHAGNUM MOSS (Spagnum palustre)

This lush moss will only thrive in a boggy spot, either in the shade or open, where it will form an attractive golden-green patch. Because it has glands that take up and retain water it is a perfect packaging for plants, and for this reason it is valued by nurserymen. It is also a rich additive to compost. During the First World War it was sterilised and used for dressing wounds, and in the distant past was used for vaginal complaints. Mixed with cresses and salt it formed a plaster for pains in the knees and thighs, and for tumours and swellings in those parts of the body. It was made into a medicine with juniper and wine to reduce the liquid accumulated by sufferers from dropsy. Farmers put it into drinking troughs as a tonic for their stock, and used it for binding wounds on animals.

SPRING SQUILL (Scilla verna) and AUTUMN SQUILL (Scilla autumnalis)

These pretty bulbous plants are to be found growing wild in southern and western coastal areas of Britain. Both roasted and raw, the bulbs were used to cure warts.

STITCHWORT (Stellaria graminea)

This common grassland plant was served as a vegetable to diabetics. Mixed with powdered acorns and wine it was drunk to ease the pain of a stitch in the side, thus its name. The juice was used to treat eye complaints, particularly those connected with diseases of the kidneys.

WILD STRAWBERRY (Fragaria vesca)

One of our most treasured wild plants, both for the charm of its white flowers, and its delicious fruit. Both the native strawberry, and its tiny European alpine cousin, have always occupied an important place in herbal medicine. It appears in a tenth-century plant list as Straberie. A tisane made from the leaves was taken to subdue fever and excessive sweating. The plant was also used for diarrhoea, threatened abortion, excessive menstruation, and as a blood tonic. Strawberry juice was used to clean tartar from the teeth, and to keep the mouth healthy. Both the juice and an infusion of the plant were used to clear up skin infections. Distilled strawberry water was mixed with white wine and drunk as a heart tonic, while the berries were recommended for gout sufferers. In veterinary medicine the herb was used for blood complaints, fever, diarrhoea and abortion.

TOADFLAX (Linaria vulgaris)

This really lovely plant with its grey-green foliage and yellow and orange snapdragon flowers, was once known as Lynary, and was widely used to treat both human and animal patients for jaundice, and complaints of the bladder and kidneys.

TORMENTIL OR SEPTFOIL (Potentilla erecta)

A cheerful little wild flower, it was used for making gargles, and treating mouth ulcers, nosebleeding, and inflamed eyes. It had a more extensive use with animals, being a treatment for gastritis, dysentery, colic, diarrhoea, wounds, sores and warts.

TWAYBLADE (Listera ovata)
This elegant, green-flowered orchid likes a shady damp spot. The powdered roots were used in salep, while medicinally it was used to treat duodenal ulcers and catarrh.

VERVAIN (Verbena officinalis)
This holy herb used to be called Simpler's Joy, which indicates the high regard in which it was held by herbalists. Legend has it that it originated from the Mount of Calvary, and for that reason was widely worn as a protective amulet. However, long before Christianity, it was used by the ancient Greeks to purify the altar of Jupiter before major festivals to the god. It was also an ingredient in love philtres, and a sprig was attached to a bride's dress to ensure the faithfulness of her husband.

Headache sufferers wore garlands of the herb, and crushed with oil of roses and vinegar, or made into a decoction with oil of roses, it was believed to prevent baldness. Herbalists, who claimed it strengthened the nervous system and sharpened the mind, prescribed it for the treatment of epilepsy, pains in the womb, old wounds, ulcers, weak eyesight, weariness, and as a gargle. Farmers used it on animals suffering from fevers, fits, convulsions, hysteria and liver complaints.

VIPER'S BUGLOSS (Echium lycopsis)
A tisane made from the leaves and stems of this handsome plant was drunk to cure headaches, while a decoction of the seeds in claret was said to produce a cheering tonic.

WILLOW (Salix viminales)
There are a considerable number of native willows, and while it is likely that the Common Osier was the one normally used, almost any found growing in swampy places could have been collected, since willow was used to treat the fevers and agues associated with swamp and marsh-land. Green, leafy willow branches were set about the bed of someone suffering from ague, because it was believed that they cooled the air.

The bark was used in the treatment of rheumatic pain, and is the source of aspirin. Burnt bark was made up into an ointment to get rid of corns, callouses on the feet, and facial spots. The leaves on their own were a treatment for gout, and also to discourage lust. According to Pliny the Elder, the leaves made into a drink 'will disable them altogether for the act of generation'.

WOODRUFF (Galium odoratum)

This thoroughly pleasing plant makes the most wonderful ground cover, and in the past was gathered in the summer and made into garlands, which were hung about the house to sweeten the atmosphere. The dried herb was put in among the linen for the same effect. Added to wine it was said to make men merry, and it certainly does impart an agreeable flavour to ordinary white wine. It was fed to animals suffering from a poor appetite, hysteria, constipation, fever, wounds, ringworm and scabies.

WOOD SORREL (Oxalis acetosella)

The pleasantly astringent leaves of this delightful woodland plant, eaten raw or in an infusion, were regarded as a good blood and liver tonic. In animal medicine the herb was used to treat fever, urinary complaints, haemorrhages, catarrh, eye problems, piles, skin diseases and wounds.

YARROW or MILFOIL (Achillea millefolium)

This very common, aromatic plant of fields and hedgerows, had a curious use among country girls. They used to irritate their nostrils with it to cause a nosebleed, which would prove that their lovers were true to them. Oddly enough it was also used to stop nosebleeding. The herb was also prescribed for headaches, diarrhoea, palpitations, excessive menstruation, piles, epilepsy and hysteria. Used fresh it was supposed to ease inflammation of old wounds. It was widely used on animals for fevers, pneumonia, haemorrhages, epilepsy, rheumatism, colic, wounds, skin complaints, earache and baldness.

Photo: 'Britain on View' (BTA/ETB)

Until recent years the Chelsea Physic Garden supplied medicinal herbs to the London teaching hospitals. The second oldest botanic garden in Britain, it held the national plant collection until that role was taken over by the Royal Botanic Garden at Kew in London.

Lilium candidum

Published by D.ʳ Woodville Sep.ᵗ 1.1791.

Photo: Eileen Tweedy

One of the oldest lilies in cultivation, and one of the loveliest, the Madonna Lily is associated with the Virgin Mary as a symbol of purity. The leaves and bulbs were used to treat many ailments, including fever and dropsy.

A gem of wood and roadside, violets have been kitchen and sickroom treasures for centuries.

Queen Elizabeth 1 used Greater Celandine to loosen her teeth before pulling them out herself.

French monarchs fought under banners adorned with the glorious iris. Its sliced roots were used to ease bruises.

A flower of childhood's golden days, foxgloves produce a vital drug for heart diseases.

Photo: John Bethell, The National Trust Photographic Librar

The herb garden at Sissinghurst Castle in Kent developed as Victoria Sackville-West's
interest in the plants developed. Because it covers a relatively large area it perfectly
illustrates how an entire garden could be devoted to herbs, without losing the colour and

form of herbaceous plants and shrubs.
Here the blue-pink plumes of Clary Sage flowers, the roses, grey foliage plants, and the rich
discs of marigolds (the 'golds' of medieval gardens) combine in perfect harmony.

Kew is a botanic garden, a scientific collection of the world's plants. It is also a garden of great beauty, and of its many features, one of the most enchanting is the Nosegay Garden; a sunken island of sweetly scented and useful herbs. The statuesque flowering heads of

angelica (right foreground) is a counterpoise to the low planting of the formal bed, while (inset) a fine clump of French Lavender *(Lavendula stoechas)* blends perfectly with the bright blue stars of borage in the foreground.

Photo: C. Henson Smith, The National Trust Photographic Library.

Walled gardens seem made for growing herbs. The tapestry colours of the flowers and leaves become enriched against a background of brick or stone, particularly those plants with golden foliage. This effect is shown to perfection in the culinary and physic garden at Acorn Bank in Cumbria.

8

Flowering Herbs
The Flowers of Paeon and the
Messenger of the Gods

What favourite flowers are mine, I cannot say –
My fancy changes with the summer's day.
Sometimes I think, agreeing with the Bees,
That my best flowers are those tall apple trees,
Who give a Bee his cyder while in bloom,
And keep me waiting till their apples come.
Sometimes I think the Columbine has won,
Who hangs her head and never looks the Sun
Straight in the face. And now the Golden Rod
Beckons me over with a graceful nod;
Shaped like a sheaf of corn, her ruddy skin
Drinks the Sun dry, and leaves his splendour thin.
Sometimes I think the Rose must have her place –
And then the Lily shakes her golden dice
Deep in a silver cup, to win or lose.
So I go on, from Columbine to Rose,
From Marigold to Flock, from Flock to Thrift –
Till nothing but my garden stones are left.
But when I see the dimples in her face,
All filled with tender moss in every place –
Ah, then I think, when all is said and done,
My favourite flower must be a Mossy Stone.

'Flowers' by W. H. Davies.

Many of the most beautiful of our flower border plants played a vital role in herbal medicine, or were valued for their cosmetic properties. Because of this the herbaceous border itself can become a herb garden, with the tall border plants forming a background to the smaller culinary and medicinal herbs. This kind of mixed gardening is particularly useful where the amount of available space is limited, and where the gardener is trying to achieve the maximum interest and variety.

The following plants, which are herbs in their own right, show that a mixed herb border will miss nothing in colour, form and texture, when compared to a flower border while providing for alternative medicine, pot-pourri, home-made cosmetics, and the kitchen.

ACANTHUS (Acanthus mollis)

Perhaps this magnificent plant should be called the Architect's Plant, instead of its more familiar name of Bear's Breeches, because its gloriously formed leaves have been the model for the decoration of great buildings for centuries. Turner says that its old English name was Branke Ursin, and he saw it growing in profusion at Syon, and said the roots and leaves were used in medicine. It was used for urinary and bowel problems, ruptures and convulsions. It was also made into poultices for wounds, abscesses and ulcers, and an infusion of the leaves was believed to purify the blood. The only problem with this perennial, which stands out in a border like a piece of sculpture, is that it can become tiresomely invasive.

AURICULA (Primula auricula)

With its fleshy, waxy leaves, one could be forgiven for believing that it was a native of some dry and arid territory. In fact its home is in the European Alps. It was introduced into this country by immigrant Flemish gardeners, and later brought to great perfection by the hybridising and selecting skills of British textile workers, to become a hugely popular Victorian florists flower. Medicinally it was used for ear troubles and vertigo.

BOX (Buxus sempervirens)

This is a classic edging plant for beds and borders, but it can also be grown into an excellent specimen plant, particularly the varieties with golden and bronze foliage. It is one of the legendary sources of the Cross, and it was believed that if you dream of box you will be ensured of a long life. An infusion of the leaves makes an excellent hair rinse.

CATNIP (Nepeta cataria)

A very good plant for both herb and ornamental beds, it has long been valued as a digestive, and is still made into a tisane for the relief of flatulence and stomach pains. It was also made into a medicine for coughs, hiccoughs and period pains.

CYCLAMEN (Cyclamen europaeum)

The tiny hardy cyclamen are one of the joys of late summer and early autumn, and certainly deserve a place in the border or herb garden. *Europaeum* is probably the species referred to in the old herbals, but coum and neapolitanum are also lovely species. Turner reported that cyclamen grew in the West Country in his time, but claimed there was no common name for them. In fact he invented one, Rape Violet, because, he argued, it had a root like rape, and flowers like violets. Interestingly he called violets, Sow-brede, and Sowbread is a name later given to cyclamen, being translated from the Latin, *Panis Porcinus*. In Switzerland the corms were used to catch trout by poisoning the fish in the streams.

Dioscorides asserted that a pregnant woman only had to step over a plant to abort, and the corms were tied about women in labour to hasten the birth. It was also used in attempts to procure abortions. In the form of a pessary it was a treatment for constipation, and the herb was also used for jaundice, made into a lotion for sunburn, and drunk with wine as an antidote to poisonous bites, and also to induce drunkenness. It was one of the many ingredients of love philtres.

DAFFODIL (Narcissus Pseudo-Narcissus)

> I wandered lonely as a cloud
> That floats on high o'er vale and hills,
> When all at once I saw a cloud,
> A host of golden daffodils;

Beside the lake, beneath the trees,
Fluttering and dancing in the breeze.

Continuous as the stars that shine
And twinkle in the milky way,
They stretched in never-ending line
Along the margin of a bay:
Ten thousand saw I at a glance,
Tossing their heads in sprightly dance.

The waves beside them danced, but they
Outdid the sparkling waves in glee:-
A poet could not but be gay,
In such a jocund company:
I gazed – and gazed – but little thought
What wealth the show to me had bought.

For oft when on my couch I lie
In vacant or in pensive mood,
They flash upon that inward eye
Which is the bliss of solitude,
And then my heart with pleasure fills,
And dances with the daffodils.

'Daffodils' by William Wordsworth.

Sadly the great wild colonies of this native narcissus are no longer as common as they were in Wordsworth's time. In the seventeenth century they grew in the meadows around London, and great bundles were brought in by countrywomen to be sold in the markets. It is a marvellous sight massed in grass. Apart from the rather harsh name, Bastard Narcissus, it was also known as Crowbells, Lenten Lily, Daffodowndilly, and Daffodilly.

Medicinally it was distilled to make a rub for massaging people suffering from palsy. It was also used for treating burns, and for making plasters to draw thorns, splinters and even arrow-heads. Apart from *pseudo-narcissus*, there are many perfectly delightful species like *cyclamineus, jonquilla, juncifolius, poeticus* and *bulbocodium*.

DAPHNE (mezereum and oleoides)

Daphne *mezereum* is a superb small shrub with sweetly scented pinky-purple flowers which encrust the leafless twigs in February and March, and are followed later in the year with bright red berries. It is rare in nature, but common in gardens, and comes easily from seed. It is used homeopathically for hayfever, and as a purge, but neither of these treatments should be attempted by amateurs. *Laureola*, which is used for the same purposes, is an attractive evergreen, often called Spurge Laurel. It has fragrant, green-yellow flowers.

DAY LILLIES (Hemerocallis)

There are some twenty species and many fine hybrids of this superb border plant. It was used to make a plaster for upset stomachs, and a linament for eye complaints. It was made into a draught to stem internal bleeding.

DIANTHUS (Carnations and Pinks)

> What was't that fell but now
> From that warme kiss of ours?
> Look, look, by Love I vow
> They were two Gelli-flowers.
>
> Let's kisse, and kisse agen;
> For if so be our closes
> Make Gelli-flowers, then
> I'm sure they'l fashion Roses

'On Gelli-flowers Begotten' by Robert Herrick.

These lovely, beautifully-scented flowers deserve a place in both herb garden and flower border. Also known as Gillyflowers or Clove Gillyflowers, they should not be confused with wallflowers, which were given very similar names in the past. They were also called Sop-in-Wine, because the blooms were steeped in wine to produce a health-giving cordial. The Cheddar Pink, which is now extremely rare and closely protected in its native home, the Cheddar Gorge, was distilled to produce a treatment for epilepsy. Plants or seed can be obtained commercially.

EVENING PRIMROSE (Oenothera biennis)

This tall, vigorous plant, with its masses of huge, primrose-yellow flowers, has almost become a native, it settles so easily into the wild. It is said to have been introduced by John Tradescant the Elder, who worked in Virginia. However, this could be innaccurate, since it is described as a native of Peru. Perhaps like the potato it made its way to Virginia before reaching Britain. Until relatively recent times it was grown and eaten as a vegetable, the roots having a flavour quite similar to salsify.

In recent years the plant, like borage, has attracted increasing interest for its oil-bearing seeds. It was the oil from the seeds which was used as a remedy for the pre-menstrual syndrome. Now, according to a report in *The Times* in 1985, it is 'an increasingly respected weapon against the symptoms of the condition'. Dr. Michael Brush, of the Department of Gynaecology at St. Thomas's Hospital Medical School, London, was quoted as saying that mood changes, food cravings and breast engorgements are all improved by evening primrose oil, although the feelings of bloatedness are less well relieved. The report did warn that the oil does not work for everyone.

GLADIOLI (G. illyricus and byzantinus)

These two species have become firmly established in parts of Britain, and, indeed, *illyricus*, is regarded as a native, although extremely rare in the wild. Known as Sword Lily or Corn Flag, they were gathered for their corms, which were made into an ointment for skin complaints and ulcers, and pounded with wine and frankincense to make a paste for drawing splinters. Also mixed with wine, the upper part of the corm was used as an aphrodisiac, while the lower part was regarded as a bromide.

GOLDEN ROD (Solidago canadensis)

I have to confess to a prejudice against this plant. It is excessively invasive, and if proof is needed just look at the railway wasteland near Clapham Junction in South London, where it grows like a forest. Handsome in the first flush of bloom, it soon becomes somewhat rank, however, a small, ruthlessly controlled clump can be found a place in the garden where it will look good. It was used to heal wounds, and for kidney complaints. It was also used to treat hay fever, although its pollen will trigger off attacks.

HELLEBORE (Helleborus foetidus)

The stinking hellebore was probably the plant used mainly by the old herbalists, but there are many other species of this extremely elegant group, which from the most ancient times has been surrounded by mystery.

It was held that if an eagle flew near anyone cutting up a hellebore, that person would die within the year. Harvesting involved a complicated ceremony of drawing a circle round the plant with the point of a knife or a sword, facing east, and praying to the pagan gods, before digging it up. Legend records that its virtues were discovered by a goatherd who noted that when his animals ate it they scoured. At the time the daughters of King Proteus were suffering from 'furious melancholy'. They were given the milk of the hellebore-eating goats and 'were brought to their right wits'.

In the past this plant, a violent purgative, was used to treat epilepsy and insanity, usually administered in milk, gruel or pottage. Boiled in oil, it was made into a liniment for headaches and dizziness.

HOPS (Humulus lupulus)

Best known in Kent and Herefordshire, where they are grown commercially for use in the brewing industry, hops, particularly the golden form, make delightful garden climbing plants. Young shoots can be eaten like asparagus, while the dried, pineapple-like flower heads have long been used to induce sleep, either in a hop pillow, or steeped in sherry for a week, and the liquid drunk at bedtime. A bag of hops soaked in boiling water and used like a poultice, eases rheumatic pains and sciatica. Hops are used to treat animals suffering from digestive problems, debility, eczema, fever and worms.

IRIS (I. foetidissima and I. pseudacorus)

These are the two native species of this marvellous group of flowers, which no garden should be without. From the most distant times it has occupied a special place in art, poetry, legend and history.

The plant is named after Iris, the messenger of the gods, who used a rainbow to travel between heaven and earth. She was also supposed to have guided the souls of women to the afterlife, and thus the ancient Greeks planted irises on the graves of women. Earlier still the Egyptians regarded it as the symbol of eloquence, and they were carved on the brow of the Sphinx, and were on the sceptres of the Pharoahs. Before Christianity, the South Slavs called it Perun's flower, after the Slavic Jove, Perun. After the Christian faith became established in Europe, the iris became closely connected with the Virgin Mary.

There is a story of a rather simple minded French knight, who could never remember more than the first two words of the Ave Maria. He retired to a monastery, where the monks cruelly taunted him for his dullness, but he was a devout man and constantly repeated the words 'Ave Maria'. When he died he was buried in the monk's cemetery, and after a while an iris grew at the head of the grave, and displayed on every petal were the words, 'Ave Maria'. The extraordinary flower induced the monks to open the grave, and they found that the roots of the plant stretched down through the soil until they rested on the lips of the old knight.

Traditionally the iris represents wisdom, faith and courage, which might well have been one of the reasons for it being adopted as the badge of the French royal family. At the time of King Clovis I of France the badge was three black toads, which attracted the attention of his enemies when he rode into battle, until a hermit living at Joye-en-Valle was brought a brilliant blue shield by an angel. It was emblazoned with three irises. The hermit took it to the Queen, Clotile, who gave it to Clovis, and from that day he triumphed in battle, although one might have thought that he would have been quite as conspicuous as before.

The iris, Fleur de Lis, was incorporated into the royal coat of arms, and after Clovis was converted to Christianity the flower became the symbol of the faith in France. Charles V chose the three flowers to represent the Trinity, and Louis VII had them on his banner during his crusade of 1137. It was said that those particular irises had appeared miraculously on his standard. The name, Fleur de Lis or Lys, did lead to some confusion over whether or not they were irises or lilies. Tasso spoke of the French golden lilies, Gigli d'oro, and in the reigns of the kings, Philip, Charles VIII, and Louis XII, the French people were called

Liliarts, and the kingdom, Lilium. The Burghers of Ghent were bound by oath not to make war on the lilies. Because of its association with French royalty, the iris was proscribed by the Revolution, and people found wearing it were executed. Napoleon substituted the bee for the flower.

The flowers, which were added to the English royal coat of arms by Edward III, were dropped in 1800, when Ireland was joined to England, and the monarchy discontinued the title, King of France.

Iris *foetidissima* is a native plant with pale purple and bronze flowers, there is also a yellow form, and most spectacular pods of scarlet berries, which sometimes can be yellow or white. It is known by a number of names; Gladden, Gladwyn, Stinking Gladwyn, and Gladwin, all derived from the Anglo-Saxon, glaedene, gladene or gladine. In Devon the berries were called Adder's Meat, or Adders Berries, and were regarded as highly poisonous. Adder in this context did not mean the snake, but was a corruption of the Anglo-Saxon word, *attor*, which means poison, thus the iris was known in Sussex as Attor-berries. Certainly, in common with many other irises, it does contain a glycoside which is poisonous to animals if eaten in sufficient quantities.

The root of the plant was used to purge phlegm, and the juice was sniffed to cause sneezing 'and draw corruption from the head'. In powdered form the root was taken in wine for cramps, convulsions, gout, stomach pains and stings. Boiled in wine, the root was used for menstrual problems, and mixed with verdigris, honey and great centaury, was made into a plaster for all wounds, but especially head wounds, and was said to painlessly draw splinters and thorns.

The Yellow Flag (Iris *pseudacorus*) is one of the loveliest of the irises when it is in full flower in marshes, and beside ponds and streams. Also a native it has attracted a number of names: False Acorus, Segg, Cegg, Skegg, Jacob's Sword, Flaggon, Meklin, Myrtle Flower, Myrtle Grass, Myrtle Root, Yellow Iris, Fliggers, Daggers, Gladdyn, Levers, Shalder, Dragon Flower and Fleur de Luce. The juice was used for persistant coughs, convulsions and cramps, as well as liver, spleen and urinary complaints. Roots were sliced and put on bruises, and mixed with sulphate of iron produced Sabbath Black, a dye used as ink in

Scotland. The flowers were made into a yellow dye.

Iris *germanica* is also known as Blue Flag, Garden Flag, Flag Iris, Common German Iris, Blue Flower de Luse, or Blue Fleur de Lys. Slices of the root were used to remove freckles, and crushed in wine was made into a medicine for people suffering from dropsy. A pessary was made from the plant with honey, and used to expel stillborn babies. Two or three teaspoonfuls were put into a cup of water and taken as a diuretic and purgative.

Iris *florentina* is a delightful border iris, and its rhizomes are a source of orris root. The roots are used in toilet water, and for the treatment of minor bruises and skin complaints. It was put, sometimes mixed with anise, among linen to perfume it. At one time the dried root-like rhizomes were made into beads to be chewed by teething babies; twenty-million a year were exported from Leghorn and Paris. Violet powder, which was sold in sachets, was made from orris root, most of it grown in the neighbourhood of Florence and Sienna. Another centre of cultivation was the village of San Polo near Parma, which produced three-hundred tons of roots in an average year. Orris powder was manufactured at Grasse, the centre of the French perfume industry.

Iris *pallida*, another lovely bearded iris, was also used as a source of orris root and orris oil, the latter being used to flavour soft drinks, candies and chewing gum, and to enhance fruit flavours in food manufacture. Both it, and *florentina* and *germanica* were used in the making of bitters, and in liqueurs of the anisette and violetta varieties. Orris was also an ingredient in toothpaste.

Iris *versicolor* is a superb iris, very variable in colour, which is found growing from Canada to Texas. It is an easy garden plant. The rhizomes were dried and used by North American Indians as an emetic and cathartic. The early settlers took the tip from the Indians, and included it in their materia medica as a purgative. They also boiled the roots and made them into poultices for burns, sores and bruises. Dried and ground iris seeds were used in America as a coffee substitute.

During the latter half of the nineteenth century, the iris was regarded as one of America's 'most valuable medicinal plants'. It was described as 'an alternative, cathartic, sialogoue, vermifuge, and diuretic', and it was prescribed for scrofula and syphilis as a 'powerful and efficient agent', as well as being useful in treating 'chronic hepatic, renal and plenitic affections'. It has a number of common names in America; American Blue Flag, Water Flag, Flag Lily, Liver Lily (it contains iridin, which is a nauseous and bitter substance that acts directly on the liver), Snake Lily, Dagger Flower, and Dragon Flower.

Iris *missouriensis* was another of the delightful American irises that was used by settlers. It is to be found from British Columbia to Mexico, and the roots were crushed and used to relieve toothache.

Like so many of the greatly valued medicinal herbs, the iris, particularly Iris *foetidissima*, was surrounded by mystic and ritual. Pliny the Elder wrote that before digging up an iris, the collector should drench the ground around the plant three times with Hydromel, a wine made from quinces, 'as though this were a sort of atonement offered to appease the earth; also, they trace three circles around it with the point of a sword, and the moment it is gathered they lift it up to heaven'.

JASMINE (Jasminum officinale)

This sweetly scented climber has been a favourite in gardens for centuries. One of its old names is Gethsamyne, and in Latin it was known as Apiaria, because of its attraction to bees. It was used to treat spots and scurf, and was laid on swellings and lumps. Oil of Jasmine was sniffed up the nostrils to cause nose-bleeding as a kind of do-it-yourself blood letting.

LADY'S MANTLE (Alchemilla mollis and alpina)

Alchemilla mollis is the most familiar species found growing in gardens, although *A. alpina* may well have been the one most commonly used by the old herbalists. Both are delightful, and never quite so pretty as when they are studded with raindrops. Once known as Ladies Mantel and Syndow, it was given to animals suffering from lack of appetite, diabetes, and heart and digestive problems.

LAVENDER COTTON (Santolina chamaecyparissus)

This neat plant with its silver-grey aromatic foliage can be used, either as an edging plant, or as a specimen plant. It was used to treat scrofulous outbreaks that affected the eyes.

LILIES (Lilium candidum)

The Madonna Lily is one of the holy herbs, and as a symbol of purity is to be seen in many of the great old master paintings of the Virgin Mary and the Infant Jesus. The bulbs were bruised and mixed with wine to counteract fever, while the juice pressed from the bulbs was stirred into barley meal and baked into cakes as a treatment for dropsy. Tiger lilies (*Lilium tigrinum*) were used in attempting to correct astigmatism. Both the leaves and bulbs of lilies were mingled with wine as an antidote to snakebite and mushroom poisoning, and cooked leaves were put on burns and wounds. Bulbs boiled in wine were made into a plaster for corns, damaged sinews, skin complaints, and to remove wrinkles. Lilies were also involved in the treatment of leprosy.

LILY OF THE VALLEY (Convallaria majalis)

This lovely flower, once it establishes itself, gives years of delight. Known as May Lily or Mary's Tears, it has a long medicinal history. The flowers were distilled in wine and given to people who had suffered a stroke. It was used for heart disease, high blood pressure, and disorders of the brain and lymph. Flowers were put in a glass container and buried in an ant's hill for a month. The liquid which gathered in the container was used externally for gout, while an infusion of the leaves and flowers was used to treat sore or scalded tongues. During the First World War the herb was an ingredient in the treatment for men who had been gassed. Animals suffering from heart complaints, and round and thread worms were given lily of the valley.

LOVE IN THE MIST (Nigella damascena)

A flower of romance, posies and cottage gardens, it deserves a place in the herb garden or border, not just because it is extremely pretty, but because it does have a culinary role. Its copiously produced seeds are lightly crushed in a mortar and mixed with ground cinnamon, coffee and chocolate, and eaten as an accompaniment to Pommel cheese, and cream.

LUPIN (Lupinus polyphyllus)

This ever-popular border flower should never be taken internally, but the seeds ground to a flour were used externally for gangrene and most skin complaints, and for cleansing the skin. It was mixed with vinegar as a balm for sciatica. Farmers used it on scab in animals.

MEADOW SAFFRON (Cochicum autumnale)

This splendid autumn flowering bulb is not to be confused with saffron, which is a crocus. Called Naked Boys, because of its habit of flowering after the lush foliage has died down, or Son before the Father, because it was thought that it produced its seed before the flower, it rose to fame medically in the eighteenth century when Baron Storck of Vienna promoted it as a popular cure for gout. It produces colchicine, a substance that increases the numbers of chromosomes. A native of Britain, it is used homeopathically for eye problems, and as a protection for eyes and ears during measles, and for skin complaints.

MONKSHOOD (Aconitum napellus)

This is a plant which should be treated with extreme caution, since every part of it is poisonous. However, with its fine foliage and deep blue flowers, it is undoubtedly very handsome. Although it was used extensively in herbal medicine, it is now only used homeopathically. Known as Wolfsbane, the roots were used to poison the meat put in wolf traps, arrow heads, and was a popular ingredient in deadly potions. Legend has it that Hecate, the moon-goddess of all the witches, used it to murder her father, and to add to its venomous image, the first plants were believed to have sprung from the vomit from the three heads of the dog, Cerberus, brought from Hades by Hercules.

PAEONY (Paeonia officinalis)

Without doubt one of the loveliest of all the flowers, the paeony has a most antique history. The ancient Greeks believed it to have been of divine origin, coming from the moon as a gift from the Goddess Diana. Alternatively there is the story that the plant was given to Paeon, a pupil of Aesculapius, the God of Medicine, by Leto, Aesculapius's grandmother, the mother of Apollo. Paeon used the plant to heal Pluto when he was wounded by Hercules during the Trojan war. What is in no doubt is that the paeony was very widely used in herbal medicine, particularly in the treatment of mental disorders and epilepsy. It was also valued as a defence against what were seen as manifestations of evil.

Dioscorides said that if the plant was picked before sunrise during the dog days and hung about the person, it would be an effective protection against poisoning, bewitching, fears, devils, fever and storms. According to Pliny the Elder, it was guarded by a bird called a Wood-speight or Hickway, which would peck out the eyes of anyone digging up the plant during daylight hours. The greatest care had to be taken pulling up the roots to avoid the collector's tiwill or fundament falling out. All told a tricky plant.

Necklets of roots and seeds were hung on children suffering from epilepsy, and a medicine was made from the roots for adult sufferers. The seeds mixed with wine were regarded as a cure for nightmares, especially the sensation of being crushed by a great weight. The roots were also used for all mental disorders, as an emetic, for convulsions and cramps, jaundice, kidney and bladder complaints, for treating wounds, varicose ulcers, rheumatism, and to expel afterbirth.

In China, the paeony was not only used in medicine, but also as a food. Animals suffering from nervous illnesses and rheumatism were doctored with paeony.

PANSY (Viola x wittrockiana)
No border should be without good patches of pansies. They are the most cheerful and rewarding of flowers. Farmers used them to treat animals suffering from pain and weak hearts.

PERIWINKLE (Vinca major and minor)
Periwinkle with its wide blue flowers and evergreen leaves is an excellent ground-cover plant, but inclined to try to take over given the chance. It is best confined to an area where it cannot bully other plants.

In the sixteenth century it was known as Clematis *daphnoides*, and it was believed that if a man and his wife ate the leaves they would be bound closer together in marriage. The leaves were also chewed to relieve toothache. It was prescribed for digestive problems, ulcers of the throat and mouth, diphtheria, diabetes, goitre, and scalp and skin complaints. Periwinkle was given to animals for haemorrhages, diarrhoea and deep wounds. *Vinca rosea*, the pink-flowered tropical periwinkle, can be grown in the greenhouse. It is used in the treatment of cancer.

ROSES

Sweet serene skye-like Flower,
Haste to adorn her Bower:
From thy long cloudy bed,
Shoot forth thy damaske head.

New-startled blush of Flora!
The griefe of pale Aurora,
Who will contest no more;
Haste, haste, to strowe her floore.

Vermilion Ball that's given
From lip to lip in Heaven;
Loves Couches cover-led:
Haste, haste, to make her bed.

Dear Offspring of pleas'd Venus,
And Jollie, plumpe Silenus;
Haste, haste, to decke the Haire
Of th' only, sweetly Faire.

See! Rosie in her Bower,
Her floore is all this Flower;
Her bed a Rosie nest
By a Bed of Roses prest.

But early as she dresses,
Why fly you her bright Tresses?
Ah! I have found I feare;
Because her Cheekes are neere.

'The Rose' by Richard Lovelace.

Of all the flowers the rose must rate as the most popular, and certainly one of the most widely used in medicine, beauty and cuisine. These are, of course, the old-fashioned roses; the Cabbage roses

(*Centifolia*), the Alba roses, of which Maiden's Blush is one of the loveliest; the Damask and Gallica, and the glorious Moss roses. The origin of the Moss roses is something of a mystery, the most likely explanation being that it is was a sport from the Cabbage rose. A little verse gives a more delightful account of its birth:

The angel of the flowers, one day,
Beneath a rose tree sleeping lay –
That spirit to whose charge is given
To bathe young buds in dews from heaven.
Awaking from his light repose,
The angel whispered to the Rose,
'O, fondest object of my care,
Still fairest found where all are fair,
For the sweet shade thou'st given to me
Ask what thou wilt, 'tis granted thee.'
'Then,' said the Rose, with deepened glow,
'on me another grace bestow.'
The Spirit paused, in silent thought,
What grace was there that flower had not?
'Twas but a moment – o'er the Rose
A veil of moss the Spirit throws,
And, robed in Nature's simplest weed,
Could there a flower that Rose exceed?'

It is the old richly scented roses that should be given a place among the herbs. In the past distilled rose water was used for heart complaints, and patients suffering from heart troubles would eat a conserve of roses in the morning and at night. Roses were also made into cordials and syrups for use as a general tonic, especially for treating fevers. They were put to use for ear problems, mouth ulcers, and mixed with vinegar to settle queazy stomachs. Swooning, fainting, catarrh, opthalmia, hay fever, and lung diseases were all treated with the flowers.

Dried roses were packed into small bags and used as a deodorant, and the ashes of roses were used to trim bushy eyebrows, although it is far from clear how this was achieved. The Romans used rose petals to flavour their wine, as well as making them into vinegar. Another lovely use of the petals is in junkets and cakes.

Originally the rose was the flower of Venus, but with the coming of Christianity it became the flower, or at least one of the flowers, of the Virgin. The shape of the rosary was said to have been revealed to St. Dominick as a chaplet of roses, and the early beads were fashioned from rose leaves that had been compressed in moulds. Sometimes they were made from the flowers.

SAXIFRAGE

There are too many saxifrages to give a specific name to any particular one, and since many of them grow in the wild in Britain and Ireland it is difficult to be certain if one or all were used medicinally. One of the most common and popular is London Pride (*Saxifraga x urbium*), and there is the white-flowered Meadow or Bulbous Saxifrage (*Saxifraga granulata*), the Purple Saxifrage, the Yellow Mountain Saxifrage, and many others. All have the virtue of being enchanting additions to the garden. They were used in the treatment of a number of eye complaints.

SNAPDRAGON (Antirrhinum majus)

These jolly annuals, which will naturalise themselves in walls and odd corners of the garden, were at one time hung up in houses to protect the inhabitants from becoming bewitched. They were also supposed to make a man gracious in the sight of others.

SNOWDROP (Galanthus nivalis)

This is the best known of the snowdrops, which are the freshest and loveliest of the early spring flowers. It is said that many arrived in this country when they were sent as love tokens by the British soldiers in the Crimea to their sweethearts and wives. It grows wild in Russia and the Balkans, and, apart from the type, there are many good hybrids and cultivars, as well as a considerable number of magnificent species. Snowdrops should be planted green just after flowering. An ointment for treating chilblains was made from the crushed bulbs.

VIOLET (Viola odorata, riviniana and canina)

This truly enchanting flower is as useful as it is beautiful. Dioscorides recommended it for sore eyes, and the flowers were steeped in water as a treatment for children suffering from epilepsy. In Tudor times it was particularly valued for bringing down fevers.

A delicious deep purple **Violet Cordial**, which was taken to ensure good health, was made from the flowers. First make a clear sugar syrup. Add a good quantity of clean flowers. Soak in the syrup for twenty-four hours, and then simmer the mixture for a short time. Strain the liquid, add more flowers, stand and simmer. This process should be repeated three or four times, before finally adding a little fresh lemon juice.

Candied violets were considered good for heart complaints, head-aches, and for light sleepers, while a conserve of the flowers and sugar was taken to settle a disturbed stomach. Other ailments treated with the plant were gall stones, gravel in the kidneys, chest and eye complaints, vertigo and catarrh. Poultices made from the pulped leaves were applied to swollen glands, tumours, goitres and boils, and garlands of violets were worn to counteract the effect of heavy drinking. The candied flowers have been used for centuries to decorate cakes, while the fresh flowers were added to salads. Salmon is made all the more appealing by serving the fish on a bed of fennel and violet flowers, and decorating the fish itself with violets. Serve with a fennel or gooseberry sauce.

WALLFLOWER (Cheiranthus cheiri)

This bedding plant of gardens and public parks, is the highly valued Wall Stock-Gillyflower, Wall Geleflours or Cheiry of the past. If you do have a wall, let them take root. When I took over my then wild walled garden in 1968 there were old woody plants of yellow and velvety-red wallflowers established in the brick walls. They are still there and never fail to produce a rich display of colour. A paste was made from the roots and used as an ointment to relieve the pain of gout, and the whole plant was made into a medicine to aid the cutting of wisdom teeth, and for pains in the sinews, muscles and nerves.

WATER LILY (Nymphaea alba)

This is the only species of this lovely flower of rivers, ponds and lakes that is native to Britain. In the past it was used as a form of birth control (or, perhaps, in certain circumstances, as revenge), since mixed in a drink, such as wine, it was supposed to render a man impotent for forty days. The root was also made into a linament and applied to the male genitals to reduce the sperm level.

WITCH HAZEL (Hamamelis mollis, virginiana and vernalis)

These shrubs or small trees are among the loveliest of the winter-flowering plants, with the naked twigs being clad with whorls of curiously shaped, sweetly scented blooms. *Virginiana* was probably the first to come to this country from where it was found in Canada and the Eastern United States, but *mollis*, from China has proved to be the more outstanding garden plant. Witch hazel is used to make a soothing lotion for all kinds of bruising and sore eyes.

WOAD (Isatis tinctoria)

Its height, handsome blue-green leaves, and plumes of tiny yellow flowers, make this a splendid background plant for both the herbaceous and herb borders. Best known as the source of a blue dye used by ancient Britons as a body decoration, the leaves were also used to staunch wounds, and for the treatment of tumours and ulcers.

9
Vegetable Herbs
Eat up your Greens

'Eat up your greens, dear' has been one of the more dreaded phrases of childhood for generations. It is scarcely surprising that so many people have grown up with a marked dislike for vegetables when one recalls the soggy, over-cooked cabbage of school slumped on a plate like rotted seaweed at the waterline, and turnips and carrots so woody there was more fun, and probably more nutrition, in chewing an old pencil.

Vegetables are crucial to a balanced diet and good health. In the past people were mystified by the fact that the impoverished Irish peasants remained remarkably free from scurvy. The explanation was simple enough; they were saved from it by being forced to survive on an almost exclusive diet of potatoes, the very vegetable that William Cobbett describes as 'Ireland's lazy root'.

The Romans recognised the virtues of vegetables. They ate prodigious quantities of cabbage in the belief that it was an aphrodisiac, when really it was just keeping them healthy, and rarely sat down to a meal that did not include a salad. Indeed the salad has been consistently popular over many centuries, and although it must have been lacking in a good deal of protein, the humble pottage sustained the poor in relatively good health.

It might seem rather curious to include vegetables among the herbs, although strictly speaking all plants are herbs, but certain of the vegetables have a genuine right to a place in the *materia medica*, and therefore in the herb garden or border.

ASPARAGUS (Asparagus officinalis)

With its delicate ferny foliage, and bright red berries, a small patch of asparagus is an attractive herb garden feature. Medicinally it is regarded as a sedative, and was prescribed for anaemia, kidney complaints, dropsy, diabetes, urinary disorders and catarrh. Syrup of asparagus, or the water it has been cooked in, was said to ease the discomfort of rheumatism. The plant was also fed to animals suffering kidney and bladder diseases.

BEETROOT (Beta vulgaris)

With its deep red roots, and red and green foliage, the beetroot is probably the most popular of the cousins of *Beta vulgaris*. Juice expressed from the leaves was used an errhine, being sniffed up the nostrils to generate a flow of mucus to relieve congestion in the head. White beet was eaten as a laxative and diuretic, and was also used to treat skin and eye complaints, and to prevent hair loss.

CABBAGE (Brassica oleracea)

The botanical name is that of the progenitor of the entire and huge brassica tribe, of which the cabbage is undoubtedly the best known. We have certain proof that the Romans ate it, and the discovery of cabbage seeds at the Bronze Age settlements in Sussex suggest pretty conclusively that it has occupied an important place in the human diet for a very long time.

Medicinally it was used to manufacture a lotion for inflamed eyes. The Tudors used the seeds in broth as a treatment for colic, and the pulped stalks were mixed with honey and almond milk for shortness of breath and consumption. The juice was taken as an antidote to fungi poisoning. Packed with sulphur, chlorophyll, calcium and phosphorus, it can rightly claim to be a truly health-giving vegetable. The Romans seethed it in cumin, salt, old wine and oil, sometimes adding pepper, lovage, mint, rue and coriander. Another method was to serve it with chopped leeks, caraway seed and fresh coriander leaves.

Two rules must always be observed when cooking cabbage: never use more than half an inch of water, and never over-cook. There are two splendid ways of cooking **Cabbage**. One is to shred it, heat some olive oil, add crushed garlic and bruised juniper berries, toss in the shredded cabbage, and stir fry. The other is to cook the cabbage in the usual way, but with caraway seeds, strain and toss in butter.

CELERY (Apium graveolens)

For eating, celery must be grown with all the care and feeding that a first class vegetable deserves. However, it is worthwhile growing one or two plants in the herb bed for the seeds, which have many uses in cooking; the Romans included them as an ingredient in a hot peppery sauce served with wild boar. They were also used in the past for fining beer. Celery seed was regarded as a carminative, and was taken to combat flatulence.

CHICORY (Cichorium intybus)

Before the days of herbicides and intensive production methods, chicory, with its blue June-sky flowers, was a common sight in cornfields. It has now become refined as an important salad vegetable, which is equally good cooked. However, the Elizabethans used it as a cosmetic, making it up into a drink to clear spotty skins, and it was also prescribed for jaundice, liver and spleen complaints.

LETTUCE (Lactuca sativa)

The most popular of the salad vegetables, it has an ancient history as a medicinal herb, although it was of little help to Adonis, who was concealed in a bed of the plants by Venus, where he was savaged to death by a foraging boar. Lettuce juice was used to treat eyes, and, indeed, it was claimed that the eagle fed on it to sharpen its eyesight. It was used as a sedative, and made into a sleeping draught, as well as being highly regarded as a bromide. The Herbalist, John Parkinson, recommended it to monks and nuns to keep them chaste, and protect them from improper dreams, and added that if it was mixed with camphor and applied to the testicles it would abate lust.

MUSTARD (Sinapsis alba)

It seems very likely that mustard was introduced to Britain by the

Romans, and has certainly been in constant use for very many centuries. Often referred to as Senvye or Senvie in old plant lists, it was employed as an antidote to snake bites and scorpion stings. Stirred into warm water it was used to induce vomiting, and mixed with cucumber juice, was a treatment for epilepsy.

Mustard baths are well-known as a means of relieving colds and chills, and the seeds were made into plasters for all kinds of aches and pains, including toothache. Mustard oil was sniffed to ease pain in the nasal cavities. A cough medicine was made from coarsely ground mustard and dried figs, boiled in strong beer. The seeds were also included in love potions. The modern, finely ground mustard powder is said to have been invented by a Mrs. Clements of Durham in 1720, but these days there is a trend towards using the whole seeds in mustards. The Italians include lemon and orange rind in their table mixtures.

ONION (Allium Cepa)

Onions can probably lay claim to being the vegetable longest in cultivation, with an unbroken history of certainly 5000 years. It is said to have been the staple diet of the slave army that built the Egyptian pyramids. It has a legitimate place in the herb garden, and allowed to flower and run to seed, it makes a handsome plant. The red onion was always regarded as the most potent. It is a strong disinfectant, and was also used to deal with persistent sneezing, hay fever and nasal discharge.

ORACHE (Atriplex hortensis)

Once known as Orech or Orege, it is now more familiar in the formal flower bed than the kitchen, although in the past it was an important vegetable, eaten as a substitute for spinach, or in salads. The red form, which is particularly striking, can reach a height of six feet. Among herbalists it had a mixed reputation. Some said that the plant, which was claimed to grow wild in corn fields, was a weed that actually caused diseases, while others recommended it for treating tumours, gout, and vaginal complaints. It was also used to produce a black hair dye.

RHUBARB (Rheum rhaponticum)

The question is, is rhubarb a fruit or a vegetable?, and the answer is that it is a vegetable eaten as a fruit. Indeed in the past it was always known as Spring Fruit. It is not a native, and there is some confusion as to its actual country of origin. Some say it is Mongolia, others Siberia, and there is a story that the first seeds to reach the West were smuggled out of China in the seventeenth century. The plant we now grow in our gardens is the result of a cross between *Rheum rhaponticum* and *Rheum undulatum*.

What is certain is that it was regarded as a sterling preventative of constipation in the eighteenth and nineteenth centuries. The Duke of Wellington never went campaigning without his rhubarb pills. These pills were delicately known as Peristaltic Persuaders, and were made from pulverised rhubarb, syrup, and oil of caraway. According to Dr. William Kitchiner, in his book, *The Cook's Oracle*, published in 1840, you had to think about the pills before taking them. 'The Dose of the Persuaders must be adapted to the constitutional peculiarity of the patient. When you wish to accelerate or augment the Alvine Exoneration, take two, three or more, according to the effect you desire to produce. Two pills will do as much for one person, as five or six will for another; they will generally very regularly perform what you wish today without interfering with what you hope will happen tomorrow; and therefore are as convenient an argument against Constipation as any we are acquainted with'.

For animals the plant was recommended for constipation and diarrhoea, gastritis, anaemia and lack of appetite. The leaves should never be eaten by humans or animals.

ROCKET (Eruca sativa)

This once popular salad vegetable should be more widely grown since it has a delicious, and distinctive flavour and mixes well with other saladings. For centuries it had a considerable reputation as an aphrodisiac, and the recommended dose was twenty leaves seasoned with salt, pepper, olive oil and vinegar. The seeds were used to make a substitute mustard. Pliny made a curious claim that an infusion of the herb in wine drunk before a whipping would render the punishment painless. John Parkinson commented that it was a pity Pliny had not tried out the potion himself, a view doubtless held by those unfortunates who tried the experiment. However a drink made from it was supposed to act as a deodorant, and it was mixed with sugar to relieve coughs in children. The seeds were given as an antidote to scorpion stings and the bites of shrews, which were considered poisonous. They were also converted into a beauty preparation with honey and gall from cattle. Plants should be kept well watered, and sown in succession to ensure a supply of tender leaves.

SEAKALE (Crambe maritima)

This delicious, but all too rarely grown vegetable, is a native of Britain, and is found growing on the seashore, particularly in Sussex and the West Country. Because it is packed with minerals, it is an extremely healthy addition to the diet. It was eaten to prevent tooth decay, as a pick-me-up for people run down after an illness, and as a treatment for rheumatism and urinary problems. It is a mild laxative. Seakale, which is a perennial, can be grown as an individual plant, or in groups in a border, and is as easy to manage as rhubarb.

10
Culinary Herbs
Herbs of Grace

How well the skilful gardener drew
Of flowers and herbs this dial new,
Where from above the milder sun
Does through a fragrant zodiac run;
And, as it works, the industrious bee
Computes its time as well as we.
How could such sweet and wholesome hours
Be reckoned but with herbs and flowers.

From: 'The Garden' by Andrew Marvell.

The delight and pleasure to be got from the great culinary herbs, must, surely, lie in their flavour and fragrance. It is impossible not to be amazed by the wonderful aromas that are released by simply pinching or brushing the foliage of these plants, reminding one of meals past, and promising those that are to come. Since the culinary herbs had, and in many cases still do have, a major role in medicine, one wonders which came first, the dish or the dose.

What is quite certain is that herbs became essential in the preparation of food from the very earliest times. It has been held that they were only used to disguise the noxious flavour of meat and fish that had either been preserved by drying or salting, or was just going bad. Perhaps there is some truth in that notion, but all the evidence of old cookery books, and accounts of ancient feasting, point to the fact that herbs and spices were used to create dishes to appeal to the palate's apparently insatiable appetite for new and enticing savours. It is hard to imagine how any cook can cope without a good and varied supply of herbs, and there are few pleasures to equal that of being able to pick your own fresh herbs, either for a favourite recipe, or to create something new and exciting.

This chapter endeavours to describe those herbs which are not only beautiful to look at, but which will bring content to the most demanding cook, as well as those which especially stand out in faith and old traditions, and the *Materia Medica* of the centuries.

ANGELICA (Angelica archangelica)

This is a truly magnificent plant either in the flower border or the herb garden. It is a native of the Alps, and is said to grow wild in Scotland, Germany, Hungary, Iceland and Lapland. At one time it was common on the Thames-side at Mortlake, and in the nineteenth century was sold from market stalls, although it is rarely seen in shops today. In the past it was known as The Holy Ghost, and there is a legend of an emperor whose army was threatened with extermination by the plague. When all seemed lost an angel appeared to him and told him to treat his soldiers with the herb. He did so and the men were saved.

The seeds were chewed as a defence against fever, and later were mixed with quinine as a treatment for fever. People who had been bitten by mad dogs, or poisonous insects, were given angelica, and the leaves were made into a tisane to ease headaches and tension, while distilled Angelica Water was prescribed for people suffering from heart disorders and fainting fits. It was also an ingredient in Lady Hewet's Water, a cure-all which was claimed to have restored people on the point of death.

Angelica gargle was regarded as a sovereign cure for sore throats and tonsillitis. Children with feverish colds were given an infusion, while the dried and powdered roots were mixed with wine to 'abate the raging lust' in young people. Just for good measure the herb was taken to aid digestion, and to relieve flatulence, colic and heartburn. With such a heavy medical demand, it is surprising that there was anything left over

107

for the table, but the young stalks were peeled and eaten in salads, or with cream cheese.

Rhubarb is given a special and delicious flavour by adding angelica leaves and stalks during the cooking. But perhaps its best known culinary use is as **Candied Angelica**, as a decoration for cakes and puddings, particularly trifles. Cut the stems in June, boil until tender, and stand in water over a gentle heat until they are a good green colour. Dry, and plunge into boiling syrup made with rose water. The leaves can also be candied.

Angelica, which was once made into a toilet water, will self-seed itself pretty freely, so there need never be any lack of plants, although they die after flowering. Plants can be made to last for several years if the flower heads are cut off.

ANISE (Pimpinella anisum)

Its feathery leaves and white flowers are an attractive asset to any herb garden, but it is not an easy plant to grow and should be started from seed under cover, with the seedlings being planted out in a warm position in May. A native of Egypt, Greece and Asia Minor, it was made into spiced cakes by the Romans, and served at the end of feasts as an aid to digestion. In France it is used to flavour the marvellous hot-weather drink, Anise, and the seeds are used in bread, cake and biscuit making. They also give a delicious spiciness to apple-pie.

Pliny the Elder declared 'be it green or dry, it serves as well for seasoning of all viands, as making all sauces, in so much as the kitchen cannot be without it'. The herb gives fish a distinctive taste and it should be finely chopped over broad beans. Wine makers in the distant past strained their wine through anise to flavour it. In medieval times, as in Roman, anise was served at the end of banquets, not as cakes, but as candied seeds. It was an aid to digestion, and to sweetening the breath.

The herb was hung about beds to make people look fresh and young, and it was stuck into pillows to induce a deep, dream-free sleep. The seeds were made up into little bags and attached under the nose to achieve the same effect. Despite its narcotic reputation, it was highly regarded as an aphrodisiac. Medicinally it was used to treat headaches, eye complaints, symptoms of epilepsy in children, respiratory diseases, gout, alcoholism, and was included in lozenges and medicines for coughs. It was put among linen to discourage moths.

BALM (Melissa officinalis)

A herb with a lovely lemon scent, it seems content to live and thrive anywhere. I have a large patch which has flourished in the shade of an old fig tree for twenty years or more. Don't let it run to seed, or it will be everywhere. Steeped in wine, it was said to drive away the deepest melancholy, and it should always be included in wine and cider cups, and Pimms.

Beekeepers believed that if the inside of a hive was rubbed with the leaves, this would keep the swarm intact. The leaves were also rubbed into wooden furniture to perfume it. Balm tea was drunk to relieve feverish colds, stomach upsets, headaches, and nervous disorders, and the old Arab herbalists made it into a tonic to restore health and strength to the elderly. Pounded and mixed with pig's fat, it was used as an ointment for bruises and wounds, and infused in wine, it was regarded as an antidote to poisonous bites. The herb was also a treatment for infertility, irregular periods, and gout. Animals were given balm for heart and nervous disorders, and for the discharge of after-birth.

BASIL (Ocymum basilicum)

It must be listed among the monarchs of culinary herbs, and yet it has enjoyed a mixed reputation, from the downright wicked to the sacred; it was mixed up with both magic and medicine, and Keats used it to adorn the tragic relic of Isabella, when she planted it in the garden pot in which she kept the head of her murdered lover Lorenzo.

> Then in a silken scarf, – sweet with the dews
> Of precious flowers pluck'd in Araby,
> And divine liquids come with odorous ooze
> Through the cold serpent-pipe refreshfully, –
> She wrapp'd it up; and for its tomb did choose
> A garden-pot, wherein she laid it by,
> And cover'd it with mould, and o'er it set

Sweet Basil, which her tears kept ever wet.

And she forgot the stars, the moon, and sun,
And she forgot the blue above the trees,
And she forgot the dells where waters run,
And she forgot the chilly autumn breeze;
She had no knowledge when the day was done,
And the new morn she saw not: but in peace
Hung over her sweet Basil ever more,
And moisten'd it with tears unto the core.

And so she ever fed it with thin tears,
Whence thick, and green, and beautiful it grew,
So that it smelt more balmy than its peers
Of Basil-tufts in Florence; for it drew
Nurture besides, and life, from human fears,
From the fast mouldering head there shut from view:
So that the jewel, safely casketed,
Came forth, and in perfumed leaflets spread.

From: 'Isabella', or 'The Pot of Basil' by John Keats.

Certainly Isabella's method of growing basil can hardly be recommended, but Keats' poem does reflect the aura of darkness and danger that surrounded the herb for so long. Culpeper described the situation when he wrote:

'This is a herb which all authors are together by the ears about, and rail at one another (like lawyers). Galen and Dioscorides held it not fitting to be taken inwardly, and Chrysippus rails at it with downright Billingsgate rhetoric; Pliny and the Arabian physicians defend it ... Being applied to the place bitten by venomous beasts, or stung by a wasp or hornet, it speedily draws the poison to it. Every like draws like. Mizaldus affirms, that being laid to rot on horse-dung, it will breed venomous beasts. Hilarius, a French physician, affirms upon his knowledge, that an acquaintance of his, by common smelling to it, had a scorpion bred in his brain.'

Others claimed that it bred snakes, or that if you chewed it and spat it out in the sun it would produce maggots and worms. The fact that goats would not eat it was taken as further proof of its harmfulness, which, popular opinion held, included harming the stomach, damaging sight, causing madness and inducing lethargy. If someone had been eating basil and was then stung by a scorpion they were given no hope of survival, and, indeed, basil was mashed up with crabs or freshwater crayfish as a bait for scorpions. And finally it was claimed that if you ate basil you would become infested with lice. Despite this dreadful reputation, in India it has always been a sacred plant, and is grown in a hollow pillar in front of Hindu houses.

Eventually physicians recognised its true worth, and it became a valuable medicinal herb. The dried leaves were used as a snuff to cure headaches, and an essence made from vinegar and basil was used to bring people out of fainting fits. It was also employed in rousing patients from comas. A liniment made with the herb, and oil of roses or oil of myrtle, was rubbed onto the temples to relieve head pains, and it was mixed with wine to treat weepy eyes. Basil was recommended for stomach complaints, flatulence, urinary troubles, jaundice, dropsy, internal ulcers, colic, warts and for drying up breasts after babies were weaned. Although it was supposed to suppress venery, it was placed on the shanks of mares and asses at mating time. Among mystics the scent of basil was regarded as an aid to meditation, although medicinally it is considered a stimulant.

But it is in cooking that basil really comes into its own. For centuries it was an essential ingredient in the soup at aldermanic dinners, and is particularly good in hare, and sturgeon soup.

In eighteenth-century French cooking it was the key flavouring in cooking mutton. A classic recipe was **Mutton Chops with Basil**. Since mutton is almost impossible to obtain these days, good lamb chops will do as well. Stew the chops in a good stock, or even some soup, with a bunch of parsley, and chopped shallots or Welsh onions. When cooked remove the chops, strain the liquid and reduce until thick. Pour the sauce over the chops and leave to cool. Make some forced meat with veal and beef, two eggs, salt, pepper, parsley, scallions (shallots or Welsh onions), and mushrooms, all chopped small and moistened with the cream and eggs beaten together with a generous amount of basil. Cover the chops with the forced meat, top with breadcrumbs, and finish off to a good brown colour in the oven.

Basil and Pigeons are an excellent combination. The birds should be stewed slowly in a stock with salt, pepper, a bunch of parsley, scallions, thyme, and a good quantity of basil, cloves, onions and some root vegetables. When they are cooked dip them in beaten egg yolks, and bread crumbs, and fry. Garnish with parsley.

BAY (Laurus nobilis)

As its name declares, this is one of the noblest herbs, both in history and appearance. It is the laurel which was fashioned into chaplets to crown Roman victors in war and the games. It was also a symbol of peace, and a branch was held up to bring about a cessation in fighting. It was also used in the most solemn ceremonies of purification before the ancient gods.

A number of old recipes refer to bay as laurel, but under no circumstances should the toxic laurel be used, any more than a herb garden should be without a bay, since the fresh leaves are so much richer in flavour than dried leaves. They should be used in cooking eels, in soups, ragouts, fish dishes, custards and milk puddings.

It was widely used in medicine. The young leaves were beaten with barley meal to treat inflammation of the eyes. Mixed with oil of iris it was used to ease headaches, and mixed with rue made a poultice to reduce swollen testicles. Two skinned berries in wine was valued for persistent coughs and shortness of breath. Alternatively the medicine was made by boiling the berries in honey and water. Bay was included in treatments for poisonous bites and stings; nearly all skin complaints; rheumatism, stomach upsets; to kill body lice, and mixed with honey it was used as an ointment for gangrene. The juice of the berries was used for deafness and ear disorders in general. Powdered bay was held to the nose to ward off the plague.

BERGAMOT (Monarda didyma)

This is quite one of the loveliest of the introductions to the herb garden from America. The flowers are a brilliant scarlet (there is a pink form), and the foliage has the most delicious scent. Posies of bergamot and southernwood used to be carried by girls and women to church. It also had an important part to play in American history. After the Boston Tea Party on 16 December, 1773, tea became a detested drink, because the tax placed on it by the British Government was a symbol of colonial oppression. The Americans looked around for alternatives. One was Liberty Tea made from the leaves of *Ceanothus americanus*. Raspberry, sage, spearmint and golden rod were used, but the most popular beverage was Oswego tea, which was made from the dried leaves of bergamot.

BORAGE (Borago officinalis)

This beautiful plant will settle in the garden, and never go away. Its somewhat invasive character is forgivable, because its apple-green foliage, and vivid blue flowers, with jet black centres, are a joy wherever they crop up. Both the flowers and cucumber-flavoured leaves can be used in salads, although it is best to strip the leaves from the stalks and chop them very fine, as they are rather rough and hairy. The Elizabethans cooked it with mutton, along with the roots of bugloss and parsley.

Its fresh, cucumber flavour is lovely in all summer drinks, especially Pimms, and it has a reputation for bringing about a sense of cheerfulness. The leaves and flowers were steeped in wine for this purpose, or alternatively it was made into a **Borage Cup**. To a quart of mild beer, add a glass of white wine, one of capillaire (a syrup flavoured with orange water), the juice of a lemon, and the thinly pared peel, grated nutmeg, a good sprig of borage, a small piece of toast, and borage flowers floated on top. Chill and serve.

The candied flowers make delightful decorations for cakes and puddings. Use the same methods as candying violets or primroses.

Borage could become important to farmers. It is now being grown commercially on a relatively small scale for the drug industry. In the past it was included in a soup with lettuce, sorrel, parsley, bugloss and chicory, eaten by wet nurses to encourage the production of milk. The leaves were also included with potherbs to ease sore throats; it was regarded as a laxative, and the fresh leaves were laid on new wounds. Herbalists recommended it for the heart, kidneys, adrenal glands and the digestive system. It was considered a cure for jaundice, and the juice was used to kill ringworm. In animal husbandry the herb was employed in dealing with rickets, digestive and nervous disorders, and heart disease.

BURNET (Sanguisorba officinalis)

This excellent herb is far too rarely grown. Not only is it extremely neat, but with its ferny leaves, and pineapple-shaped pinky flower heads, it is very attractive, and a refreshing addition to any salad. Its cucumber-flavoured leaves should be stripped from the stalk, and finely chopped. It is a native plant, and not difficult to grow, although I found that my original bought plant did not do nearly as well as its self-sown progeny; so leave it alone to scatter itself. It is also widely distributed throughout Europe, and a Hungarian legend tells of King Chaba, who, after a particularly bloody battle, cured the wounds of fifteen thousand men with the juice of the plant. According to Middle Eastern magicians, the blades of newly forged swords should be steeped and tempered in the juice of burnet, mingled with the blood of moles.

Although it was one of the ingredients in a complicated recipe for a medicine designed to heal internal wounds, and the leaves were pulped to make a dressing for external wounds, it is more reliable as a culinary herb, especially in the creation of refreshing summer cups. Like borage, it has always been regarded as a merry herb when it is mixed with wine, particularly claret. The leaves should be bruised before being added to the drink. It is also a very good soup herb.

CARAWAY (Carum carvi)

This is a tough, easily grown biennial, which is invaluable in the kitchen. Its feathery foliage and umbels of white flowers are an attractive feature of the herb garden. It can be chopped into a salad, used in cooking fish, and added to stews, soups and stuffings.

A native of Siberia, Iran, the Himalayas, and many parts of Europe, it is also believed to be indigenous to Britain, although the probability is that it was introduced to this country by the Romans. Certainly they used the herb in most of their sauces, and caraway seed was cooked with cabbage to give the vegetable flavour.

The root can be eaten as a vegetable, but this is almost unheard of these days, and it is the seed which is the vital part of the herb. In medieval times, roasted apples and caraway seeds were served at the end of meals, and this dish was traditionally produced at Trinity College, Cambridge. It seems probable that the apple, Caraway Russet or Fenouillet Gris, was used for this purpose.

In Germany, Holland, Czechoslovakia and Russia, caraway seeds are used to flavour stewed mutton, mashed turnips and soups. They also make an excellent vinegar, and are invaluable in bread and cheese making. Indeed, ground caraway seed mixed with a little sugar and sprinkled on bread and butter is a classic accompaniment for gorganzola cheese. **Seed Buns** are made by mixing caraway seed with plain bun dough. Set in a warm place, and before baking brush with beaten egg white and dissolved sugar. Bake for ten minutes.

Medicinally the seeds were believed to be good for the digestion, and as a mouth freshener. They were also bruised and mixed with new bread and a little spirit to make a poultice to ease earache, and they were an ingredient in Dr. Steven's Water, a seventeenth-century preparation, basically made from ginger, which was supposed to prolong life and cure all ills.

CHAMOMILE (Anthemis nobilis)

Strictly speaking this is not a culinary herb at all, but on the other hand no herb garden would be complete without it, although it was registered as a pot-herb in the fifteenth century. However, chamomile tea is valued as an agreeable tonic, and its rich green leaves and bright white flowers are always a pleasure. While chamomile does not make a successful lawn, it is a very attractive edging to a border or bed, and is a delightful top for a turf seat. Medicinally it has a long history, being used to treat fever, jaundice, neuralgia, tumours, ulcers, exhaustion, and worms. At one time it was prescribed as a substitute for quinine. The dried flowers were smoked to relieve asthma. Made into a lotion, it helps to produce a clear complexion, and as a rinse it is said to lighten the hair. Farmers used it to treat their animals for blood and skin disorders, constipation, and internal and external inflammation.

CHASTE TREE (Vitex agnus castus)

This somewhat tender shrub is essentially a medicinal herb, but is so attractive it deserves a place in the herb garden. Over the centuries it has acquired a number of different names: Monk's Pepper, Abraham's Balm, Agnus Tree, and the English Hemp Tree. This latter name comes from the fact that the leaves are very similar in appearance to cannabis, which used to be grown in Britain for the manufacture of cordage. The leaves have a pleasant spicy scent, and could well be added to pot-pourri. In powdered form it was given to soldiers and monks as a bromide, and Athenian women strewed the herb on their beds during feast times when they were supposed to remain celibate. Maidens who wished to remain chaste slept on a bed of the leaves and flowers. The seeds were believed to prevent conception, and the herb was also used to treat dilated pupils.

CHERVIL (Anthriscus cerefolium)

This is one of the great classic herbs, and essential to *fines herbes*. People are put off by its habit of rapidly running to seed and producing relatively scant foliage. This is overcome by sowing in the late summer, then it will produce leafy plants which will stand through the winter, and very satisfactorily take the place of parsley. A native of the Caucasus, Western Asia, and South and Central Russia, it is excellent in soups, and was an essential ingredient in a thick, meaty gruel, known as Loblolly. A winter tart was made with the herb in the eighteenth century. The old herbalists regarded chervil as an anti-depressant, a good tonic for the elderly, and a stimulant to the brain. According to Pliny the Elder it was the perfect pick-me-up for tired lechers. He declared that if a man had exhausted himself with a surfeit of women, then chervil would restore his spirits. As for old men, he vividly comments: 'Yea and such as be wel stept in yeares, and begin to droup, it maketh lusty and able to perform the act of generation youthfully'.

It was chopped over soups as an aphrodisiac, and for this purpose there is a recipe for **Moules à la Mariniere**. Put very well cleaned and scrubbed mussels into a saucepan with some butter, chopped shallot, parsley and chervil. When the mussels open over the heat pour in a glass of dry white wine, add a little more butter, and freshly ground pepper. Garnish with chopped parsley and serve.

The fresh leaves are excellent in salads, or mixed with mustard and cress as a side salad. The green seeds used to be eaten with oil, vinegar and pepper. Eaten either raw or cooked, chervil is said to be good for the stomach, and a decoction was recommended for complaints of the bladder, kidneys and liver.

CHIVES (Allium schoenoprasum)

The neatest of all the onion tribe, chives are grown for their grassy leaves. Finely chopped they give a delicate onion flavour to salads, and certainly no potato salad is complete without them. Eaten with bread and butter as a sandwich, they are an excellent tonic. To ensure a steady supply of greenery never allow the plants to flower. However, if you have more than enough clumps, let one or two bloom as they will produce a pleasing splash of pale purple among the other herbs.

CLARY (Salvia sclarea)

This splendid robust plant must be planted either at the back of a border, or in the centre of a bed. With its grey-green leaves, which sometimes seem to take on a blue bloom, and the masses of misty pinky-purple flowers, it is outstandingly striking. The specie plant is much more elegant than the rather garish hybrids which have been produced for bedding. Clary is a diminutive for Clear-eye, and true to its name it was widely used for eye complaints. Also known as Oculus Christi, the seeds were placed in the corner of the eye to attract foreign bodies. They were also steeped in water to produce a thick mucilage, which was used for soothing and clearing the eyes. It also had a reputation as an aphrodisiac, and was included in a brew made from the marrow from the backbone of a cow, ale, catmint, stoned and sliced dates, raisins, and whole nutmeg. This disgusting drink had to be swallowed last thing at night.

Clary Wine, on the other hand, was drunk to aid sleep. For this you had to mix thirteen pounds of sugar with ten gallons of water, and the well-beaten whites of sixteen eggs. A pint of clary flowers, complete with small leaves and stalks, was put in a barrel with a pint of brewers yeast. The liquid, which had been boiled for an hour, being constantly skimmed, and left to stand until quite cold, was poured in, and stirred twice a day until it stopped working. The barrel was sealed, and the wine left for four months before bottling. In Germany, the wine, in which elder flowers had been infused, was used to adulterate muscatel. The herb was used in beer brewing to give the drink extra strength and to ensure a good head.

Clary also produces one of the few vegetable fixatives for perfumes. The leaves, used quite sparingly, are good in stews, stuffings and soups. Dipped in batter and fried, they make **Clary Fritters**, which were regarded as being particularly beneficial to people in ill-health. Tender leaves were beaten with cream, fried, and served with orange or lemon-flavoured sugar. Young leaves, finely chopped, can be added to salads.

COMFREY (Symphytum officinale)

This is a plant which has gone through a modern revival as the ultimate health herb, a claim which has been challenged by some experts, who have accused it of being carcinogenic. However, it will settle in an odd corner, and look very good. In the past it was known as Blackewurt, and an infusion was used both internally and externally for eye injuries. Master John Gardener listed it among the essential kitchen garden plants at the time when the herb and vegetable garden were blended. Whether or not it was a genuine potherb is not clear, but it is certain that its tonic virtues have long been valued.

To make a strengthening tonic in the eighteenth century, the roots were scraped and boiled (a pound to three pints of water) until the liquid was reduced to a pint. This was strained, and once cooled was mixed with half a pint of white wine and the juice of a lemon, re-boiled, and strained into an earthenware pot for keeping.

The leaves were used in the setting of bones, which gave it its old names of Boneset, Knitbone and Bruisewort. They were also made into poultices. Organic gardeners greatly value the plant in the production of compost.

CORIANDER (Coriandrum sativum)

This is one of the oldest and most valuable herbs, which must have been introduced into this country by the Romans. Its decorative leaves look well in a mixed green salad, and also make a delicious **Coriander Sauce**, chopped up with mint and cucumber, and mixed with yoghurt. Coriander seeds, which have a slight flavour and aroma of tangerines, were sugared and eaten as sweetmeats, with roasted apples at the end of meals. The seeds are an aid to digestion. But it was also claimed that if the herb was eaten to excess it would derange the mind.

Meat that was powdered or corned and mixed with coriander and vinegar was said to remain eatable throughout the summer months. A more sinister use was to mix it with fennel, and burn the two as an incense to summon up evil spirits. A preparation, Eau de Carmes, which was invented by Carmelite monks in Paris at the beginning of the seventeenth century, had coriander as an essential ingredient. It was drunk as a cordial and also used externally as a toilet water. It was made from two pounds of balm in flower stripped from its stalks, four ounces of fresh lemon peel, eight ounces of coriander seeds, two ounces of bruised nutmeg, cloves and cinnamon; one ounce of dried angelica root, and ten pints of highly rectified spirit. The seeds are used to produce *Oleum Coriandri* for flavouring, and for use in the perfume and soap industry. Medicinally it was used to treat erysipelas (St. Anthony's Fire), and over-florid complexions. It was made into a plaster to treat chilblains, and ague.

COSTMARY (Chrysanthemum balsamita)

Alecost, Mace, Little Balsam, Balsamint, Mawdelin, Maudlin and Cost were all names given to this once popular herb. Originating in Western Asia, it was used extensively by the Romans, particularly in making sauces. No doubt they brought it to Britain, where it remained in cultivation by the Saxons, and was used by the Normans as an ingredient in a sauce for fish dishes. The Elizabethans used it with meat, and in salads and sauces, but by the sixteenth century it began to disappear from gardens. There seems no logical explanation, since it is an attractive plant, with its blue-grey leaves, and filmy yellow flowers, and its habit of holding its leaves through the winter, it makes a valuable mint substitute. It will produce a very passable 'mint' sauce for lamb. In the past it was mixed with lavender to give a sweet, fresh smell to linen.

The leaves were boiled with parsnip seeds to make a medicine for upset stomachs, and the foliage made into a conserve with sugar, was eaten by people suffering from catarrh. The herb was a purge for worms, and used to treat urinary complaints, sores and ague.

CUMIN (Cumin cyminum)

With the growing interest in Indian food, this delightful little herb is becoming increasingly familiar. Its richly spicy seeds are an ingredient in curry powder, but are also used on their own for flavouring oriental dishes. The Romans used it in many of their recipes, including the somewhat unappetising sounding stuffed wombs. They frequently combined it with rue and leeks, and in sauces for vegetables, especially marrows and cucumbers. They used the seeds in dressings for strong meats such as wild boar and ostrich, as well as with the more normal mutton, lamb, beef, veal, and shell fish. It seems very likely that they brought it with them to Britain, and it was certainly grown in Saxon gardens, and used in a chicken broth during medieval times.

A sauce for cabbage was made from cumin, salt, old wine and oil. It was mixed with coriander, leeks and raisins, thickened with flour, for beets, carrots and parsnips, and with honey, vinegar, liquamen, defrutum and oil for turnips.

DILL (Anethum graveolens)

This lovely, feathery-leaved plant has reigned in the kitchen and nursery for many centuries. Dill water was, and still is, a gentle carminative for babies and very young children, and, indeed, its Saxon name, Dillan, means to lull or soothe. The Romans mixed it with aromatic salts to aid digestion, and included it in particularly rich dishes. The seeds were boiled in wine as a cure for flatulence, and chewed to stop hiccoughs. In New England they were called Meeting Seeds, because women armed themselves with a packet of the seeds, when they went to chapel, to get themselves through the interminable, and frequently indigestible sermons. They were supposed to stimulate the brain, but perhaps they simply made the tedium bearable.

Leaf tips and seeds were boiled in milk to increase the supply of milk in nursing mothers and wet nurses. When oil was substituted for water, the mixture became an aphrodisiac, but some herbalists claimed that the herb caused impotence, and dimmed the eyesight. Dill, which was burnt as an incense by the ancient Greeks, was an important weapon in the defence against witchcraft, and was supposed to be the antidote to poison administered by witches and sorcerers.

But the herb is at its finest in cooking, especially the preparation of fish, with either the foliage laid on the fish during cooking, or made into a green sauce. Lamb stews, and most other stews, are greatly improved by it. In medieval times it was grown specifically for pottage. This probably went back to Roman days, when it was used in a thick broth made from barley, lentils, peas, chick peas, coriander, fresh leeks, fennel and fennel seeds, beet, mallow leaves, young cabbages, lovage and oregano. It should be used in bean soups, and cooked with broad beans, and always when pickling cucumbers (the famous dill pickles), and cauliflower. In Russia the finely chopped leaves are scattered over salads and boiled potatoes.

ELECAMPANE (Inula helenium)

This is such a splendid, statuesque plant, with its huge pale green leaves, which look as though they should be growing in a jungle, and its towering stems and bright yellow flowers, that no herb garden or border would be complete without it.

It is an ancient herb, which has acquired a number of names: Ploughman's Spikenyard, which is wholly inaccurate; Little Helen, from the legend that Helen of Troy's hands were full of its leaves when she was abducted by Paris (another version says it grew from her tears), and Horseheal, from its widespread use in treating horses, especially making poultices.

Medicinally its most important role was in treating coughs, asthma, and consumption, for which its roots were employed. Various methods were used to make it more palatable. It was dried, powdered and mixed with syrup. It was boiled in vinegar, or eaten with raisins and dates. A confection was made with quinces, service berries or plums, with the rather odd addition of pepper or thyme. Candying was a favourite method. The roots were scraped and thoroughly washed, and cut up into pieces before being boiled until they were soft, when they were pulped and mixed with their own weight in sugar or honey, and spread on a tray to set.

Elecampane was taken to counteract fainting fits, and as a treatment for upset stomachs. According to Pliny the Elder, the Empress Julia Augusta never let a day pass without eating a little of the root. Boiled at the rate of a quarter of a pound to three pints of water will produce a tonic which should be taken four times a day. The hairs of the root applied to a snake bite were supposed to stop the spread of poison, as was a drink made from the roots. The leaves were boiled in wine as a treatment for sciatica.

FENNEL (Foeniculum vulgare)

One of the aristocrats of the herbs, fennel was used by the ancient Chinese, Indians, Egyptians, the Greeks and the Romans, in both cooking and medicine. The Romans included it in a wide variety of sauces, such as one with rue, mint, coriander, pepper, lovage and honey, macerated in oil and liquamen, for serving with globe artichokes. Sauces made with the seeds were eaten with chicken and boar. In Ancient Greece the herb was believed to impart strength, and garlands made from it was used to crown victorious warriors and athletes.

Like dill, it is excellent with fish, which were wrapped in the leaves to keep them firm. An infusion was used for boiling fish, especially mackerel, which was also served with a fennel sauce. It is an essential ingredient in all eel dishes. Also, like dill, it was eaten by American church-goers, who took sprigs with them to nibble during the lengthy sermons. It, too, became known as 'Meeting Seed', and was possibly eaten to subdue thoughts of food, because in medieval times huge quantities were consumed by the poor to reduce hunger pains, and by the fat and over-fed as a slimming aid.

John Evelyn valued it as a salad herb, peeling the young stalks and treating them like celery, or serving the leaves chopped and dressed with oil, vinegar and pepper. As a relish it was used as **Pickled Fennel**. First bring salted water to the boil, tie the fennel in bunches and scald. Lay the bundles on a cloth to dry. When cold pack into jars with a little mace and nutmeg, fill with cold vinegar, put a sprig of green fennel on top, and seal.

Florence fennel, which forms 'bulbs' just above the root, makes a delicious **Fennel Soup**, which is regarded as an aphrodisiac. Boil the 'bulbs' in a good stock, liquidise, and return to the heat with the addition of a generous measure of cream. Serve with fried croutons.

The juice of fennel was mixed with wine to flavour medieval broths.

In the past blind people ate the herb in the hope of restoring their sight, from the myth that blind snakes ate it for this purpose, and that all serpents slept in the shade of fennel to strengthen their vision. Fennel water was used as an eye wash, and the plant was employed in the manufacture of eye medicines and ointments. The stalks, which are a mild laxative, were eaten to help insomniacs to sleep.

Fennel was used to treat snake and dog bites, to ease stomach pains, to increase fertility in men, for smallpox and measles, and combined with husked barley as a stisane for kidney disorders. An infusion of the seeds was taken for coughs, and it was mixed with lily-of-the-valley to help people recover from strokes. Sorcerers burnt it as an incense during the sinister ceremonies for raising evil spirits. Farmers fed fennel to animals suffering from eye and gastric ailments, worms and constipation.

FEVERFEW (Chrysanthemum parthenium)

This compact little chrysanthemum is a very pretty addition to the herb garden, particularly the golden leaved form. Its neat white flowers have given it the alternative name of Bachelors' Buttons.

Feverfew is an effective pain killer. The bitter leaves, which have something of the taste of wintergreen, eaten fresh will cure headaches, and migraine sufferers have found that a few eaten every day will go a long way towards controlling attacks, although it should not be regarded as a cure for the condition. Some people are allergic to the herb, so it should be taken with great caution at first.

It used to be prescribed to reverse infertility; to aid labour, release afterbirth, and also to prevent abortion. People suffering from dumbness and depression were treated with feverfew, as were those suffering with the ague, quotidian fever, and cramp. The foliage was made into cooling poultices. The plant was considered a good tonic for animals, and an aid to digestion.

FOXGLOVE (Digitalis purpurea)

Apart from its great beauty, the foxglove is one of the most important of our native medicinal herbs, although not one to be tinkered with by amateurs. However, it should have a place in a truly representative herb garden.

It has been used by herbalists since ancient times, was described in the first century AD by Dioscorides, and was employed extensively throughout Italy during the Middle Ages. The poor used to make the leaves into an intoxicating tea, which must have been extremely dangerous, and in general it was regarded as a bit of a cure-all, with compresses of the foliage being used to ease headaches, reduce tumours, and relieve inflammation; but it was not until the eighteenth century that its true value began to emerge.

Dr. Erasmus Darwin, father of the great Charles Darwin, published the first scientific account of its virtues. However, the real credit should have gone to Dr. William Withering, who practised in Stafford, and really put digitalis on the medical map. A graduate of Edinburgh University, one of the subjects he loathed was botany, although later in life he was to become the author of a standard botanical text book. It is said that his interest in botany was stimulated by a Miss Helena Cookes, a flower painter, who was one of his patients. When she was ill and housebound, he collected the specimens she needed for her work, and far from being a chore, his plant-hunting expeditions became a great pleasure. In 1772 they were married, and he moved his practice to Birmingham, but continued to make a weekly trip to the Stafford Infirmary.

Three years after his marriage he heard of a cure for dropsy, which was the secret of an old Shropshire woman. It produced violent vomiting and was powerfully diuretic. Although twenty or more herbs were involved, the main one was foxglove, and it seemed to him that it was the only really active ingredient. Withering embarked on a long series of experiments, using foxglove to treat dropsy. His problem was working out dosages, since too much digitalis can kill. The break-through came when Dr. Darwin called him in to see a dropsical woman patient, who was desperately ill. He treated her with foxglove. She rid herself of eight quarts of liquid, and recovered her health. During the course of his work, Withering also discovered that digitalis was a valuable herb in the treatment of heart disease. He was a modest and generous man, who was only too eager to share his discoveries. Indeed, it was he who sent foxglove seed to America, so that it could be cultivated as a medicinal herb.

While its main use has been in the treatment of cardio-vascular disease, in the 1960s it was discovered that it was useful in remedying glaucoma, the eye complaint which leads to blindness, and in dealing with detached retinas. It has also been used for muscular dystrophy. It was made into poultices for tumours and swellings in animals, and as an external pain reliever.

GARLIC (Allium sativum)

Not only is the kitchen quite bare without garlic, but if one is to believe all the claims made for it, it is the very prop and stay of life itself. In fact it comes as quite a surprise to discover that it does have a minus side. It was said to dull the eyesight and cause windiness. It leaves one feeling a little like Jerome K. Jerome, who, suffering from a touch of hay fever, decided to diagnose his ailments from a medical dictionary in the Reading Room of the British Museum. He discovered that he was suffering from every known disease and malady, except housemaid's knee. 'I felt rather hurt about this at first; it seemed somehow to be a sort of a slight' he wrote in *Three Men in a Boat*. 'Why hadn't I got housemaid's knee? Why this invidious reservation? After a while, however, less grasping feelings prevailed. I reflected that I had every other known malady in the pharmacology, and I grew less selfish, and determined to do without housemaid's knee'. So it seems we must put up with garlic's small imperfections.

Culinary garlic has been found growing wild in Siberia, but whether or not that is its native home is a matter for conjecture. If so it certainly travelled south many centuries ago, since it was grown and eaten in great quantities in the Egypt of the Pharaohs, by the Israelites, and the Greeks and Romans.

It was valued as a defence against the powers of darkness. Garlands

125

of the flowers were draped about casements to ward off vampires, and the plant was used to defeat the evil eye, and destroy the influence of witches. However, wild garlic (*Allium ursinum*), also known as Wood Garlic, Ransoms, Ramsey, Bucrames, Rames and Sauce-Alone, was used by witches and magicians in so-called magic potions.

Pliny the Elder described it as a powerful antidote to all kinds of poisoning, from that of monkshood, to scorpions, spiders and insects. It would, he claimed, counteract the bites and stings 'of venomous beasts', and to this end could be eaten, taken as a drink, or applied as a liniment. The use of garlic to treat haemorrhoids, known in the distant past as Serpents, was as unpleasant as it was curious. The patient had first to eat a large amount of the herb, and then drink quantities of wine until it caused vomiting. Turner spoke of three garlics in use in his time. Two, the common culinary garlic, and wild garlic, were grown in gardens, while the third, Crow Garlic (*Allium vineale*) was gathered from the fields and woods.

Garlic was used externally to kill skin parasites, and internally as a tonic, building up resistance to germs, improving the blood, and feeding the brain. But it didn't end there. According to the herbalists you could use it for chest complaints, worms, leprosy, the bites of shrews and mad dogs, removing afterbirth, head ulcers, the King's Evil, madness, as a gargle, for toothache, dandruff and headlice, catarrh, headaches, cramp, boils, ague, bruises and stripes caused by blows, shingles, for drawing splinters and the ends of broken arrows, as an aid to sleep, and crushed and mixed with green coriander in strong wine it 'increaseth the heat of lust, and provoketh Lecherie'.

And if that was not enough, it was considered excellent for treating poultry, horses and donkeys suffering from fever, lung and skin complaints, gastric trouble, rheumatism, liver fluke, mange, ringworm, ticks and lice. The juice of garlic diluted with water was used to check the supperation of festering wounds, and it was put to this purpose during the First World War.

One great objection to garlic is the smell it leaves on the breath. Various tips are given to overcome this. One is to remove the green core from the clove, another is to chew parsley, or eat roasted beetroot, after eating garlic or garlicky food.

Its use in cooking is universal; in French dressing, soups, especially hare soup, stews, with rosemary for roast lamb, and with all kinds of pasta, as well as Chinese and Indian food. In medieval times garlic sauce was served with haddock, codling and pike.

In the distant past the cloves were planted in small hillocks of earth. However, the simplest method of cultivation is to plant the cloves nine inches apart in January or February in four-inch deep trenches filled with well-rotted manure.

WHITE HOREHOUND (Marrubium vulgare)

With its grey-green foliage lightened with a down of fine white hairs, this is a pleasing plant for the herb garden or border, and a useful treatment for colds. Indeed, it is claimed that if you eat a few of the very bitter leaves every day you will never catch a cold. Horehound Syrup was taken for both coughs and colds, and at one time in the country, Horehound Beer was a regular brew. A tisane can be made from the dried leaves, and for asthma sufferers it was recommended to make a medicine from the dried leaves boiled with honey. The herb, which seems to do best when it is allowed to self-seed, was used for treating jaundice, consumption, bites from snakes and mad dogs, to clear the eyesight, for earache, eczema and shingles. Mixed with vinegar, it was a dressing for ringworm. It is also mildly laxative, diuretic and a vermifuge. Animals were treated with horehound for coughs, pneumonia, bronchitis, tuberculosis, and other lung complaints, ear problems, diarrhoea and liver disorders.

HORSE-RADISH (Armoracia rusticana)

No herb garden should be without this robust plant, if only for making real **Horse-Radish Sauce**, not the insipid mixture sold in jars. Wash and scrape the roots, and grate, or better still, because they are even crueller to the eyes than onions, put them through a food processor. Mix with single-cream, white wine vinegar, sugar and a little salt. Stand for an hour or so before use.

While it is still eaten with smoked mackerel, in the past it was used far more extensively in fish cookery. Eighteenth-century cooks always put horse-radish and salt in the water they used to boil fish; lemon and horse-radish were used to garnish boiled salmon, and scraped horse-radish and parsley were crisped and eaten with baked cod's head. It was mixed with sweet herbs and used in cooking carp, and was an essential flavouring with skate. While it is better known as an accompaniment to beef, in the eighteenth century it was served with roast leg of mutton stuffed with oysters. Bruised horse-radish roots were put into wine to turn it into vinegar.

Medicinally it was used for renal complaints and dropsy, and a teaspoon of grated root spread on bread and butter was eaten daily in the belief that it would reduce internal growths and ulcers. As it is an antiseptic, it was used to make poultices, and employed in the treatment of sciatica. Spirit of horse-radish was taken for dyspepsia, and to stimulate the appetite.

HOUSELEEK (Sempervivum tectorum)

Once known as Jove's Beard and Sengrene, the habit of growing it on roofs came from the belief that it was a protection against thunder and lightning, however, it will do just as well on the ground. In fact in ancient times it was grown in pots and pans outside houses.

The young, tender leaves were put into salads, but it was normally grown as a medicinal herb, being an essential ingredient in green ointment, which also included rue, wormwood, chamomile, balm, ground ivy, the inner part of elder bark, mullien, and celandine, mixed with cream, pig's fat and butter. It was boiled in milk to ease fevers, and the juice was mixed with honey for sore throats. Simmered with cream it was made into an ointment for St. Anthony's Fire. It was also used in the treatment of scalds, sores, shingles, external ulcers, canker, the cutaneous disease, tetter, ringworm, warts, corns and eye complaints. The herb was mingled with milk or honey and drunk as a blood tonic. Farmers used it in dealing with bruises, ulcers and eye problems among their stock.

HYSSOP (Hyssopus officinalis)

This neat, sub-shrubby plant is a real beauty in the herb garden, with its narrow leaves, and lovely deep blue flowers. A native of Southern Europe, it is extremely hardy, with only the very ends of the twiggy branches being trimmed by the frost. In fact the plant does need pruning otherwise it will tend to become straggly.

One of the sacred herbs, bunches of it were used for sprinkling holy water and in cleansing ceremonies. The Romans used it in cookery, and combined with other herbs in the aromatic salts they took as digestives. The Saxons used it in pottages and sauces, and also as a distilling herb. Because it is bitter it should be used sparingly, but it is an excellent addition to stews and stuffings. Very finely chopped or powdered, it can be scattered over a salad for its tonic effect. In the seventeenth century, when fish was close to going off, it was laid on a bed of rushes, and covered with fresh hyssop and winter savory.

In medicine it was used to regulate high and low blood pressure, for the relief of catarrh, as a calmative, and for bringing out a fever. Mixed with honey, salt and cumin seed, it was a treatment for adder bites, and an infusion of the chopped leaves and stems was a lotion for inflammation and bruising, especially black eyes. It was made into a shampoo for getting rid of head lice. Animals were given hyssop for coughs, sore throats, pneumonia, worms and eye disorders.

LAVENDER (Lavandula spica)

This is the familiar old English lavender, without which no garden, let alone a herb garden, is complete. The Romans used it to scent their baths, a practice which has been passed down the centuries. The extraordinary freshness of lavender is why lavender water is a perennially popular perfume, and nothing can quite match lavender bags among clothes and linen. *Lavendula stoechas*, the French lavender, has a particularly strong scent, but the plants are somewhat tender. The compact 'Hidcote' form of *spica* is especially suitable for small gardens, and there are also the charming white and pink flowered forms.

The herb was used as a nerve tonic and a cough cure, and as a mouth wash it was believed to keep the gums healthy and be a defence against halitosis. Tincture of lavender, rosemary, crushed cinnamon and nutmeg was dabbed on the forehead to ease headaches. Flowers mixed with cinnamon, nutmeg and cloves, and ground to a fine powder, were mixed with distilled lavender water and taken as a medicine for heart ailments. Palsied people were bathed in distilled lavender water, and an oil made with the flowers and olive oil was used as a rub for the complaint. The oil from lavender can be extraced by suspending a bunch of flowers in a bottle stood in direct sunshine. The plant was fed to animals suffering from vomiting, nervous complaints, foul mouths and loose teeth.

LIQUORICE (Glycyrrhiza glabra)

This is a hardy plant grown for its roots, although it does produce attractive blue, pea-like flowers. It is best known through the sweets, Pontefract cakes, but in the past it was widely used in medicine to restore loss of speech, to staunch bleeding, to heal wounds; for piles, ague, liver and stomach complaints, and scabies. Mixed with passum, it was used to quench the thirst, and when made into lozenges it was regarded as a cure for colds.

According to an eighteenth-century French recipe the way to make the lozenges was to put a pint of river water into an earthenware pot with a pound of green liquorice, scraped and cut into small pieces, two handfuls of barley, and four golden pippins. Boil slowly for four or five hours until the whole mixture has been reduced to less than a pint, liquidise, add a pound of sugar and two ounces of melted gum adragant. Boil until the ingredients become thick and sticky, pour on to an oiled tray, and when cold cut up into lozenges.

LOVAGE (Levisticum officinale)

This grand and ancient herb is far too little grown these days, and yet it is the most delicious addition to soups, stews, sauces and stuffings. It can be easily raised from seed, but the simplest method is to get a good, firm crown, which will soon develop into a fine clump.

It was one of the major Roman herbs, and was included in the classic Lucanian smoked sausage made from meat and fat, pepper, cumin, savory, rue, parsley, leeks, mixed herbs and laurel berries, which, more probably were bay berries. It was used in a wide number of dressings for vegetables, and fungi, and in sauces for meat, poultry and shell fish. Oysters were served with a sauce of lovage, pepper, egg yolk, vinegar, liquamen, oil and wine. Since it was so important to Roman cookery, it seems very likely that they introduced the plant to the British Isles. It was certainly grown in Saxon gardens, and was cultivated by the monks as a medicinal herb, but by the mid-seventeenth century it had disappeared from most gardens although it was grown in physic gardens.

The very young shoots, leaves and the green seeds can be used in salads. The shoots should be peeled. Its distinctive celery flavour is delicious in soups, stews and stuffings, and the dried seeds can be used for flavouring and for making an excellent vinegar. Medicinally it was used for treating jaundice, and a whole range of stomach disorders, for convulsions, and for sweating out fevers. It was part of a cordial, which also included tansy, and a type of milfoil (*Achillea ligustica*), commonly sold in pubs many years ago.

Lovage oil, which was distilled from the roots, was used for flavouring, to a small extent in making perfumes, and in certain tobacco mixes. An infusion of lovage was used as a skin cleanser.

MALLOW (Althea officinalis)

This is a prolific family, but *officinalis* was the one grown in herb and physic gardens. It is a charming plant with rosy-purple single flowers. At one time the young leaves were a common ingredient in salads, although that use has long been out of fashion. It was also valued as one of the most potent of medicines. Pliny the Elder, who did make a number of remarkable claims, asserted that if a man or woman drank a small quantity of the juice 'of any mallow' they would be free of all diseases and live in perfect health. Pliny also persuaded his readers that the powdered seeds were an alarmingly powerful female aphrodisiac, if scattered upon the genitals. 'She will be so forward after the company of a man, and she will never be satisfied nor contented with embracing' he wrote. Another remarkable claim made for this herb was that if the leaves were beaten up into a pulp in oil and smeared all over a man he became 'unstrikable'.

Less exotic uses were as a shampoo to deal with scurf and head sores; for toothache, and to set loose teeth; for treating wounds, urinary problems and the King's Evil. Mixed with goosefat it was said to procure an abortion, and it was certainly used to speed up a birth. The leaves were put on bee and wasp stings, and boiled into a broth with the root to induce vomiting in someone who had been poisoned.

MANDRAKE (Mandragora officinarum)

Probably the most magical and sinister of all the herbs. Known as Madrage or Madrag, Devil's or Satan's Apples, and Eordhaeppel (Earth Apple) in Anglo-Saxon, the forked root was supposed to resemble a human form, despite the fact that normally the roots are a carroty tap, and utter a terrible shriek when wrested from the soil. Anyone who heard the sound would die, and for this reason dogs were used to pull the mandrake. If you did decide to dig up the plant without the aid of a dog, special precautions had to be taken. You must never have the wind blowing in your face, only on your back. Three circles had to be drawn round the plant with the point of a sword, and then it was lifted facing the west.

While it was taken as an aphrodisiac by the elderly, its principle use was as an anaesthetic. In the most ancient times it was given to patients who were to undergo cauterising or cutting operations to dull the pain. In some cases it rendered people totally insensible for up to four hours, but since it is a very toxic plant, this must have been a hazardous practice.

Dioscorides said that the shepherds ate the fresh leaves to make them sleep, which is extraordinary since normally the leaves were pickled in brine before use to render them less poisonous. It was also used for treating cholera and eye complaints. Another claim is that if ivory is boiled with mandrake roots for six hours it becomes soft enough to be fashioned like clay.

MARIGOLD (Calendula officinalis)

There is no need to seek for an excuse for including marigolds in the herb garden, simply because they are such bright and cheerful flowers, and of course they have a place there from their long history as both a culinary and medicinal herb. They have been known by a number of different names, such as Golds, Yellow Golds, Mary Buds, Mary Gowles, Ruudes, and among Celtic people as the Flower of Mary. The petals were used to decorate salads, in soups, stews and stuffings, either dried or fresh, and can also be candied. They are also used to colour and flavour cheeses.

Charles Lamb was not an enthusiast. He recalled, with loathing, the boiled beef on Thursdays at Christ's Hospital 'with detestable marigolds floating in the pail to poison the broth'. A lotion made from the petals was used for sprains and wounds, and also for oily skin. While a salve or ointment made from them was regarded as good for the complexion. Marigolds were considered a source of disinfectant for treating internal and external ulcers, and taken regularly it was claimed they would ease catarrh. A conserve made from the flowers and sugar was taken daily by people suffering from heart complaints, and the herb was used to cure warts, eye injuries and deafness.

Animals were fed the herb when they were suffering from vomiting, internal ulcers, fevers, heart and skin complaints, eczema and warts.

MARJORAM (Origanum vulgare)

Perhaps the sweetest of all the herbs, particularly the Sweet, or Knotted Marjoram (*Origanum majorana*), it should always be part of a *bouquet garni*. Also known as Dittany, there is a legend that the original Marjoram was a page at the court of King Cinyras of Cyprus who, one day, dropped a jar of rare perfume. He was so overcome with terror that he collapsed and was transformed into the scented herb. The botanical name, *Origanum*, means 'joy of the mountains', where people encouraged it to grow on graves to ensure the dead happiness in the after-life.

Curiously the Romans did not make much use of it in their cooking, except as a sauce for bulbs, which was regarded as an aphrodisiac dish, but it was widely grown in medieval Britain as a pottage herb. It was also used as a strewing herb; to perfume baths, and put in bags amongst linen. With flowers, mint and rue, it was made into nosegays.

Although by the nineteenth century it was slipping out of favour as a culinary herb, in the seventeenth century, **Marjoram Pudding** was still a popular dish. Take the curd of a quart of milk finely broken, a good handful or more of sweet marjoram chopped as small as dust, and mingle with the curd of five eggs, three egg whites, beaten with rose-water, some nutmeg and sugar, and half a pint of cream. Beat all these well together, and put in three quarters of a pound of melted butter. Put a thin sheet of pastry at the bottom of your dish, then pour in your pudding. Cut out little strips of pastry the breadth of a little finger, and lay them over in large diamonds; put some small bits of butter on the top, and bake.

Marjoram should always be used in hare, and sturgeon, soup.

As well as being essential in the kitchen, it was highly valued in the physic garden, being used to treat snake bite, ruptures, spasms, convulsions and dropsy. Mixed with honey it became a cough medicine, and in milk, drops for earache. The herb was blended with pitch to make a plaster for chilblains, and dried and ground into a snuff to stop sneezing. It was made into an emetic by being boiled with onions and left for forty days before use. Marjoram was used in poultices to treat wounds caused by poisoned weapons, and to draw splinters of wood and bone. Animals were given the herb for digestive problems, catarrh, nervous disorders, and wounds.

MINT (Mentha spicata)

This is Spearmint, which is probably the most commonly found mint in gardens, but there are many other varieties which have been cultivated in herb gardens for centuries, such as Peppermint, Apple Mint, Curly Mint, Variegated Mint, Lemon Mint, Pennyroyal, and those with old names, which make them difficult to identify in many cases: Cross Mint, Holy Mint, Our Lady's Mint, Brown Mint, Brook Mint and Heart Mint.

Roman cooks made tremendous use of mints. Pennyroyal was used to dress cucumbers and melons, while garden mint was used with pepper, lovage, rue and coriander in flavouring cabbage. In the seventeenth century, it was an important ingredient in all salads, and mint sauce was a common accompaniment with most meats, and not just lamb. Indeed, the scent of mint was used to stimulate people and give them an appetite. As a sauce it was eaten with mackerel, especially in East Anglia. Mint was one of the regular strewing herbs, and was also used to scent baths, and was thought not only to invigorate the bather, but also to clear up any skin complaints.

The most important medicinal mint was undoubtedly, Pennyroyal, also known as Pudding Grass, because of its inclusion in hogs pudding, Run-by-the-ground and Lurk-in-the-ditch. Powdered Pennyroyal was used to sweeten stale and stagnant water, and to discourage mosquitoes, while medicinally it was used in a liniment for a whole range of aches and pains, and made into a decoction to calm itching. Mixed into a drink with honey and salt, it was taken for lung complaints, Ashes of the herb were rubbed on the gums to harden them. People suffering from nausea were given a mash made from the mint, salt and barley, while people suffering from cramp and convulsions were rubbed with pennyroyal, salt, vinegar and honey. It was used to treat stone and gravel, gout, and dumbness, and to abort stillborn babies, and the fresh plant was held under the nose of someone in a faint to bring them back to their senses. Animals were given the herb when they were suffering from digestive problems, coughs, pneumonia, bronchitis, and pleurisy. The Italians believed that it would protect them from the Evil Eye, and in Sicily garlands of Pennyroyal were hung from fig trees to prevent the fruit falling before it ripened.

Good use was made of the other mints. The wild Corn Mint was used to prevent milk from curdling, while the bruised leaves of Peppermint were laid on the forehead to cure headaches. Chaplets of mint were worn to prevent giddiness and fainting fits. The juice of the herb was believed to kill worms, and mixed with the juice of a pomegranate was considered a cure for hiccoughs and vomiting. Mint was employed in treating earache, breast swellings, and, possibly internally, as a female contraceptive.

In Roman medicine it was highly regarded as a remedy for leprosy. It was first chewed and then the masticated leaves were laid on the leprous parts. Legend had it that a leper, trying to disguise the evidence of the disease, smeared himself with mint juice and was cured. A drink made from the herb was given to women after childbirth, and it was prescribed for breathlessness, and all types of poisoned bites and stings.

Arab herbalists valued it as a means of enhancing virility, combating impotence and reviving a flagging libido, a thought to keep in mind when making the refreshing summer drink, **Mint-Ale**. Take one cup of orange mint, apple mint and spearmint, and mix with a pint of water, two tablespoons of sugar, the juice of an orange and a lemon, and a large bottle of ginger ale. Use plenty of ice and garnish with sprigs of apple mint.

MYRTLE (Myrtus communis)

This attractive bush or small tree is sensitive to very severe cold, when even well-established plants may be cut to the ground. Although as they often break again from the base, it is worthwhile having one in the herb garden. Like the bay, it is associated with courage and nobility of spirit. After the Romans and the Sabines made up their differences, the soldiers laid down their arms and were purified with myrtle. It was burnt as an incense, and triumphant generals were crowned with chaplets made from the sprays of its ever-green foliage.

Myrtle became known as Venus's Tree because it was often worn at weddings, and, indeed, Queen Victoria had myrtle blossom in her bride's bouquet. A walking stick made from a branch was supposed to ensure that a traveller would never suffer from fatigue or boredom.

The Romans made a popular drink from bruised myrtle berries steeped in wine, which was also taken as an antidote to fungi poisoning. Oil of myrtle was used to clarify wine. As a flavouring, the berries are excellent in rice puddings, and with cooked fruit. In the past they were chewed to sweeten the breath. Dried and powdered leaves were used as a dusting powder to prevent excessive sweating, and for piles and chilblians, while the whole dried leaves were employed in treating ulcers. Ashes of the leaves were a dressing for burns. The plant also provided a black hair dye, and a treatment for dandruff and thinning hair, as well as medicine for heart disease, measles, jaundice, urinary problems, and bleeding gums.

NASTURTIUM (Tropaeolum majus)

This colourful flower used to be known as Indian Cress, Cresse, or Kerse, and was much more widely used than it is now. Both the leaves and flowers can be included in salads, and the leaves on their own in sandwiches. The large green seed heads are an excellent pickle, and make a good substitute for capers. In the eighteenth century the flowers were used with parsley to garnish potted tongues used to stuff boned chickens, which in turn were stuffed into a boned goose. After it was cooked the goose was potted in butter and eaten cold. The leaves were valued as a tonic, good both for the blood and the digestion, and the juice was used to treat nasal polypi.

PARSLEY (Petroselinum crispum)

One of the true ancients of the herb garden, it has held a central place in cooking, culture and medicine from very early times. While many herbs have gone in and out of fashion, parsley has remained consistently popular, and is one of the very few herbs sold fresh in greengrocers.

A symbol of strength and courage, Hercules chose it as his personal plant, and it was used to make garlands for the victors in the Nemean Games, a Greek festival held at Nemea in the second and fourth years of each Olympiad. The Greeks also planted it on graves, and the expression 'to be in need of parsley' meant that a person was close to death.

There seems to be a great deal of argument about the precise time when it was first introduced into Britain. Some authorities insist that it was not cultivated in England until the reign of Edward VI in the mid-sixteenth century, and yet it seems inconceivable that this native of Southern Europe, which was so extensively used in Roman cuisine, was not brought to Britain earlier, especially as it is a perfectly hardy plant. Between 1330 and 1400, William Longland wrote of peasants growing parsley, and the Normans made a sauce for fish from parsley, sage, costmary, dittander, thyme and garlic.

The Elizabethans cooked meat balls with parsley, as much to colour them green as to flavour them, and the roots were boiled with mutton. The seeds, either on their own or mixed with fennel seeds were a flavouring for cheese, and this was one of the reasons why Charlemagne ordered it to be grown in his gardens. As well as being cooked as a vegetable, parsley roots were included in relishes made from pears and quinces, while the juice of the plant was used as a food colourant.

Catherine de Medici is credited with introducing parsley to France in 1533 when she came to marry Henry, second son of Francis I, King of France, but it is clear that it was being grown and used as a flavouring herb in that country long before that time. Parsley was used with boiled venison, and stewed beef. A stuffing that goes back to medieval times was made by parboiling the herb in pig's fat or sheep suet, and mixing it with chopped hard-boiled egg yolks, pepper, ginger, cinnamon, saffron, salt, grapes and cloves. Sometimes onions were substituted for grapes. A sauce was made with finely chopped and ground parsley mixed with vinegar, a little bread and salt, and then strained. Cold whelks were served on a bed of parsley soaked in vinegar. A traditional ingredient in moules mariniere, the herb is also used in sturgeon soup.

Green Parsley Paste will keep well in a sealed jar in the refrigerator, and makes an unusual sandwich filler. Bone and wash two ounces of anchovies. Boil a large handful of parsley in an open pan for five minutes. Cool under cold water, and strip from the stalks. Chop very fine and blend with the anchovies and a quarter of a pound of butter. Pot and seal.

Parsley can be an awkward and patchy germinator, which gave rise to the belief that the Devil takes his tithe from the seeds. Off-putting for men is the claim that a man who successfully grows the herb is a failure in bed, and, indeed, the plant was regarded as distinctly male and female, the female ones having the curled leaves. If a man or woman ate the stems of the female parsley, it was said they would be rendered sterile. Women breast-feeding babies were forbidden to eat any part, because the herb was thought to cause epilepsy in infants.

Of the many rules for sowing the seeds, one was that this should take place on Good Friday. Another that the soil should be soaked with boiling water. For speedy germination it was recommended to steep the seeds in vinegar, and plant in a bed strewn with the ashes of bean-water mixed with the best aqua vitae, and finally covered with a woollen cloth. On top of all that it was considered extremely unlucky to transplant seedlings, or meddle with the plant's roots, as this would bring disaster upon the grower, his house and family.

Farmers treated their animals with parsley for kidney and bladder problems, worms, rheumatism, sciatica, neuritis, and arthritis. The roots were used for constipation, and the seeds for colic and fever. They also regarded it as a defence against footrot in sheep. As recently as the nineteenth century, in Hampshire and Buckinghamshire, sheep were grazed on parsley for two or three hours a week to improve the flavour of their flesh. The plant was also grown in pastures to attract hares.

PURSLANE (Portulaca oleracea)

This was a far more important herb in the past than it is now, but its pleasing red stems and tiny yellow flowers add colour to the herb garden, and its succulent leaves are excellent in salads. As it is a little tender it should not be sown until the late spring.

At one time it was scattered on beds to ward off evil spirits, which, at the dead of night, might creep up on people deeply asleep. It was recommended as a treatment for burns caused by lightning or gunpowder; an antidote to poisoned arrows, the bites of venomous spiders, monkshood poisoning, and carried to prevent scorpions from stinging. Other medical uses were for headaches, rheumatism, ulcers, dropsy, eye and gum complaints, and haemorrhoids. It is rich in vitamin C, and in the past was taken as a tonic.

ROSEMARY (Rosmarinus officinalis)

Grow for two ends, it matters not at all,
Be't for my Bridall, or my Buriall.

'The Rosemarie Branch', by Robert Herrick.

This lovely and holy plant is most certainly a herb of grace. It is the herb of remembrance, of which poor, sad, mad Ophelia said: 'There's rosemary, that's for remembrance; pray, love, remember . . .', and, indeed, it was, from the time of the old Arab herbalists, prescribed as a restorative of strength, memory and speech. It was also carried at funerals and cast upon the coffin as a mark of remembrance, and exchanged by lovers as an emblem of love and loyalty. Holiness was attributed to it from the legend that the flowers were white until the Virgin Mary threw her mantle over a rosemary bush, whereupon the flowers were transformed to blue, the same blue that is such a joy in the late winter and early spring.

In medieval times the plant was grown very extensively, often being trained to a height of ten feet or more against walls, despite the assertion that no plant ever exceeds the height of Christ when he was on earth. It was also said that where rosemary flourishes the household is ruled by the woman.

An ingredient in Eau-de-Cologne, it was, with distilled water, made into Hungary Water, a lotion said to have been especially devised for Queen Elizabeth of Hungary, to, according to some authorities, cure her of paralysis, and to others to rid her face of wrinkles. Certainly the leaves and flowers boiled in water produce a liquid which is a very good face rinse. It should be allowed to dry on the face, and is claimed to keep the skin youthful throughout life. Many people still use it as a hair rinse and scalp lotion. It was used to put the green into pomatums, and is said to prevent hair from uncurling in the rain, and was put among clothes and linen to discourage moths.

The Elizabethans made toothpicks from the wood, and used ashes of rosemary to clean their teeth. People chewed the roots to relieve toothache, and put the juice from the leaves on offending teeth. With figs and sage it was steeped in wine until the liquid was absorbed, and then the heated fig was held against aching teeth. A decoction made with wine was supposed to whiten black teeth.

Mixed with pepper and honey, it was taken for coughs; garlands were worn around the head to clear stuffiness; it was made into sugar lozenges to ease heart complaints. Herbalists also used it to deal with menstrual pains, as a heart and liver tonic, to reduce high blood pressure, to treat jaundice, calm nervous disorders, and it was burnt to ward off fever.

The herb is invaluable in cooking. There can, for example, be few more delicious joints than roast lamb sprigged with rosemary and garlic. It should always be used to flavour hare soup, and at one time was a popular seasoning for beef. **Rosemary Sauce** is served with baked red mullet. Melt one and a half ounces of butter in a frying pan and fry a sprig of finely chopped rosemary. Add one ounce of flour and mix well. Put in a pint of stock, the juice of a lemon, and a tablespoon of anchovy sauce. Boil rapidly for ten minutes. In the seventeenth century a stock for cooking pike and carp was made from rosemary, parsley and thyme, with the addition, sometimes, of gooseberries and barberries.

Used very sparingly it is an interesting addition to a salad, makes an excellent vinegar, and goes well in stuffings. With olive oil and garlic, it is a superb marinade for chicken pieces, which should then be grilled, barbecued or cooked at a high heat in the oven. Bee-keepers value the herb, and farmers used it to dose animals suffering from heart disease, fits, rheumatism, diarrhoea, wounds and falling hair.

RUE (Ruta graveolens)
Its name is a corruption of Ruth, which means repentance, remorse and

sorrow, and led it to becoming known as the Herb of Grace, or the Herb of Repentance. In the Christian church it was used for sprinkling holy water, and in exorcism rituals; but long before Christ, mythology tells us that Mercury gave it to Ulysses to help him reject the charms of Circe and her potions. It was revered and valued by both the Greeks and Romans, and by the Druids.

Rue is, indisputably, one of the loveliest of the herbs with its rich blue-green foliage, which seems to take on a glowing quality in the winter, and its clear pale gold flowers.

Although the Romans used it to make a sauce to go with flamingoes, and vegetables; in stuffings, and as a salad with vinegar and salt, it was all but dropped as a culinary herb centuries ago. Many people are put off by the strong and distinctive aroma of the crushed leaves, but a very small quantity finely chopped imparts a delicious flavour to a green salad.

However, its principle use has always been for healing, and as Pliny the Elder said: 'Rue is an herb as medicinable as the best'. John Gerarde in his Herbal quotes several verses in praise of the herb. One says:

> It stays the cough if it be drunk,
> It cleanseth monthly flowers,
> If you seeth in water, and
> Thereto put wine that scours (vinegar);
> Such broth doth stay the belly gripes.
> It helpeth breast and lung;
> It cures the sickness of the sides,
> Called plurisy in Greeks tongue.
> The gout and the sciatica,
> And agues it doth cure,
> If it be drunke: and other things,
> As writers do assure.

The leaves were considered a good tonic, and were often pickled and eaten as an aid to health. An infusion of a teaspoon of the freshly gathered herb in three-quarters of a pint of water was taken in small quantities for cramp, bad veins, sciatica and rheumatism. Heated in the dried rind of a pomegranate, the juice was a treatment for earache.

141

Mixed with a little water the juice was always stored in a copper or brass flask.

Seeds steeped in wine were regarded as an antidote for poisoning, and although a poison in itself, if taken in excess, rue was valued as an anti-toxin, particularly against monkshood and fungi, the stings of scorpions, bees, hornets, wasps, the bites of snakes and mad dogs, and those of lizards, salamanders and shrews, which were falsely believed to be venomous. Its reputation as a defence against snake bite came from the widely held opinion that weasels ate it before attacking serpents. It was planted around buildings to keep out reptiles, and scattered at the entrance of chicken runs to discourage predators, particularly cats and fulmers, and as an additional protection against cats, the juice was sprinkled on the poultry. A drastic and never to be attempted 'cure' for rue poisoning was a dose of hemlock, itself a source of poison traditionally used for execution or suicide.

Engravers, carvers and painters used to eat rue, confident that it would sharpen their vision. Both Leonardo da Vinci, and Michelangelo daily bathed their eyes in rue water. It was also mixed with honey and fennel juice for the same purpose. The Romans put it into new wine, and used it to induce second sight. Rue was infused in wine to make a draught to cure headaches, and an infusion of the leaves was taken before a heavy drinking session to stave off drunkenness.

As a guard against the plague, and to keep away disease-carrying flies, it was planted in window-boxes in towns and cities. Judges included it in the bouquets they carried during sessions, and it was strewn on the floors of courts to ward off the fever and vermin brought from the prisons by the defendants. In addition to all this it was made into a liniment with vinegar and oil of roses; eaten with figs for dropsy; prescribed for shortness of breath, coughs, ague, chills, madness, heart and internal complaints, removing afterbirth, carbuncles, chilblains, bloodshot eyes, worms, and for getting rid of old scars. It was boiled with hyssop for stomach upsets, crushed and put up the nose to stop bleeding, mixed with oil and wine for frostbite, and chewed to kill the smell of garlic or onions on the breath.

It was widely held that if it was eaten by a pregnant woman it would destroy the child in the womb, and both Dioscorides and Pliny asserted that it was a contraceptive. Dioscorides wrote that if it was eaten or drunk it 'extinguisheth geniture'. Pliny was more explicit. He declared that if it was eaten with ordinary meals it 'should disable folke as wel in the act of generation, as conception: In which regarde it is prescribed unto them that shall shed their seed: and unto such as use to dream in their sleepe of amatorious matters and the delights of Venus'.

Often applied through the nostrils, it was given to animals for poisonous bites, broken wind, fever, hysteria, epilepsy, neuralgia, heart problems, worms and skin parasites.

SAFFRON (Crocus sativus)

This beautiful and valuable crocus, once known as Safforne, owed its genesis, according to legend, to a tragedy. A youth, Crocus, was playing quoits with Mercury, when he was killed from a blow on the head. The first saffron crocus, so the tale tells, sprang from the blood from his fatal wound. Until the end of the eighteenth century it was grown commercially in England, first at Saffron Walden in Essex, to which it gave its name, where it was introduced by Sir Thomas Smith during the reign of Edward III. Later it spread to Herefordshire, Hampshire, Cambridgeshire, and is also said to have been cultivated on Saffron Hill in Holborn in London, an area once rich in gardens, although it seems more likely that it was a trading centre for the product.

According to Brian Mathew, the Kew botanist, and a leading expert on the crocus, it was quite a tricky crop to raise. It needed rich, heavily manured land. Up to thirty loads of well-rotted dung to the acre were ploughed in three times before planting. Following that a man with a narrow spit-shovel dug a shallow trench into which the corms were planted by women, at the rate of 392,040 to the acre. Ideally the land should have carried a crop of barley, and after two crops of saffron the fields, they rarely exceeded three acres, were left fallow for a year. The flowers were gathered in the early morning before they opened, and the long scarlet style was picked out and dried over a fire.

The first corms are supposed to have been smuggled into England in a hollow staff carried by a pilgrim during the fourteenth century. Wherever it was that he acquired them it was illegal to take them out of that country, but which country is not clear, although the plant is to be found growing in Italy, Greece, Iran and India.

During the Middle Ages there were terrible punishments for people who adulterated saffron with marigold petals, or any other substance. The counterfeiter was either buried or burned alive. The Romans used the seeds of the Autumn-flowering crocus as a vegetable rennet in cheese making. In Germany it was made into tiny balls with honey, thoroughly dried and then powdered and sprinkled over salads.

A favourite recipe from the past was Dishel, a mixture of saffron, eggs, grated bread and sage boiled up together. Topers made a draught from the herb to take before drinking bouts in the hope of avoiding drunkenness, and wore chaplets of saffron on their heads for the same end.

In medieval cooking it was put into chicken broth, and was widely employed as a food colouring. It is good in hare soup, and essential in bouillabaisse, and Cornish saffron cakes. In fact it is one of those herbs which spans continents, being as important to Asian cuisine as it is to European. Sir Francis Bacon held that the use of saffron in broths and sweetmeats was what made the English a sprightly race in his time.

Medicinally it has always played an important part, being credited with reviving people close to death, and being a powerful aphrodisiac. It was used to restore weak limbs, and to regulate the liver; made into a liniment, and mixed with fennel and milk to protect the eyes from the effects of smallpox, or made into an eye treatment with raw eggs. Combined with aloes and celandine, it was taken to improve the eyesight. Herbalists used it for snake bite; to induce sleep; for ulcers, and to treat consumption, inflamed ears, and toothache. Saffron tea was an old 'cure' for measles, and a toddy of brandy or rum, sugar, and a pinch of saffron in a pint of hot water was drunk to ease flatulence and spasms. A little of the herb is still put in the water of caged birds for their health, and to improve the colour of the plumage of canaries. In the past it was used as a hair dye.

SAGE (Salvia officinalis)

An historic herb which has stood the test of time and taste. While the Romans, according to Apicius, do not appear to have made any use of it in their cooking, it was employed by the Greeks and Arabs, and was certainly grown in Saxon gardens. It was valued as a distilling herb and as a source of medicines, and various tonics that went under, according to the recipe, the names of sage tea, or wine, or ale. When the Catholic Church was the national rite, a paste of sage, parsley and butter spread on bread was allowed during the fast periods.

Its enduring popularity was for a long time based on the fact that it was regarded as an aid to longevity. One antique endorsement declared that '. . . from the beginning of taking it will keep the body mild, strenghten nature, til the fulness of your days be finished; nothing will be changed in your strength, except the change of your hair; it will keep your teeth sound that were not corrupted before; it will keep you from the gout, the dropsy, of any swellings of the body.'

Travellers used to tie sprigs of sage to themselves so that they would never be weary, or think the distance too great.

With its grey-blue leaves, the common sage is a handsome plant in the herb garden, which should also include the red sage, and the variegated sage. All three seem to have been considered equally effective in the kitchen and the sickroom, although most of the old herbals tend to come down on the side of red sage. In cooking it is invaluable in stuffings, and for flavouring rich stews, sausages and cheeses. In the eighteenth century a little butter and sage was worked into the gravy to go with roast pork, and finely chopped, with pepper and salt it was used to fill the cavities of ducks and geese before roasting. Stewed beef was flavoured with sage, and a green sage sauce was served with the little freshwater fish, loach, which were cooked in a broth. The herb was put in with calves heads when they were being boiled, and also mixed with the brains, vinegar and pepper to serve with the head. A garnish for roast pig's brains was made with sage and currants. The flowers and very young leaves were added to salads.

Bunches of the herb were put in among clothes and linen to keep them moth-free. Medicinally it was used for coughs, colds, headaches, fevers, liver, bile, the digestive system, and as a lotion for external ulcers, sores and skin complaints. A poultice was made with the leaves of red sage, hot ash and vinegar to relieve the pain of a stitch. In medieval times it was prescribed to soothe the nerves, and still trembling hands. It was also thought to drive away fever. Cosmetically it was made into a black hair dye. Sage was given to animals suffering from nervous debility, paralysis, gastric complaints, eczema, fever, wounds, bruises and hair loss.

ST. JOHN'S WORT (Hypericum perforatum)

The Perforate St. John's Wort, is just one of the many species of this attractive plant. It is particularly common, especially on chalky soil, and so may well have been the one most likely to have been gathered by the simpling women. Also known as St. John's Grass, this lovely group of plants has long held a place in medicine and ritual. As has already been described it occupied a central position in the midsummer rites, because it was considered to hold powerful magical properties that were feared by all evil spirits. The rusty spots to be found on the stems were said to be the blood of John the Baptist. On the Isle of Man there is a legend that says that it you step on the plant after sunset you will be carried off all night on a fairy horse.

It was used as a painkiller for people recovering from operations, and used externally to treat burns, scalds and minor wounds. Hypericon Oil was valued in dealing with spinal injuries, and a decoction of the herb in wine was taken to fight fever. The herb was also administered for sciatica, and people suffering from insanity and melancholia. St. John's Wort was given to animals suffering from coughs, chest and lung infections, rheumatism and worms.

SAVORY – SUMMER SAVORY (Satureja hortensis): WINTER SAVORY (Satureja montana)

Both of these splendid little herbs are at last coming back in to more general usage. Summer savory is a tender annual, and rather like Sweet Marjoram, has a finer flavour than its hardier brethren. Winter savory is the tough brother; a wiry perennial sub-shrub, which forms neat bushes, with the aid of a little pruning, and bears lovely blue flowers.

The Romans used it in sauces and sausage making. It was grown in Saxon gardens, and the Elizabethans used it as an anti-flatulent with peas, beans, rice and wheat. It should always be included with broad beans during cooking, and is excellent in pork pies, sausages, stuffings, and as a flavouring in pea soup. At one time trout was dressed with a handful of savory, sliced horse-radish, rosemary and thyme.

In the nineteenth century **Savory Jelly** was a popular accompaniment for meat, poultry and fish. Take veal, ham and lean beef, and put them in plenty of water, with a good bunch of winter savory, two carrots, two turnips, and three onions. Boil slowly until the liquid is reduced and strong. Strain, skim and season with white and cayenne pepper, and salt. Add the juice and parings of a lemon, a glass of wine, a glass of mushroom ketchup, and the whites of six eggs. Boil for six minutes. Pass through a jelly bag until clear. Store in jars.

Savory was used in a very simple and inexpensive soup known as **Green Meagre Soup**. Put celery, two or three carrots, a turnip or two, and a pound of split peas into boiling water with a good knob of butter and a large sprig of savory. Boil for an hour and a half, and strain. Rough chop parsley, spinach, chives or young onions, and chervil. Boil them in the stock. Season with a pinch of mixed spices and salt. Serve with fried breadcrumbs.

The herb was taken to improve the sight, and the leaves were applied to wasp and bee stings.

SORREL (Rumex acetosa)

There are few more useful herb garden plants than the big-leaved French sorrel, and a group of six plants or so will keep the average family well provided for for many years. The sharp flavour of the leaves, which inspired my children when they were young to call it sour cabbage, and eat it fresh from the bed, is delicious in salads. Indeed, John Evelyn, did not consider a salad to be complete without it, remarking in Acetaria that it '. . . aswages Heat, cools the Liver, strengthens the Heart; is an Antiscorbutic, resisting Putrefaction, and imparting so grateful a quickness to the rest, as supplies the want of Orange, Limon, and other Omphacia (oil or sour grape juice), and therefore never be excluded'.

In medieval times sorrel puree was used as a flavouring, and as a colouring. It was also used as a rennet to sour milk, and for making a form of verjuice. French cooks in the seventeenth century stuffed sole with the herb, buttered and grilled the fish. Another old recipe, with the engaging name of **Salamongundy**, which used sorrel, was made from two finely minced chickens, which had either been boiled or roasted; an alternative to chicken was veal. Chop separately the yolks and whites of hard boiled eggs. Shred the flesh of two or three lemons. Lay in a dish a layer of minced meat, a layer of yolks, a layer of whites, a layer of anchovies, a layer of lemon, a layer of sorrel, and a layer of spinach, topped with finely chopped shallots, and garnished with scraped horse-radish, barberries, and sliced oranges and lemons. This confection was served as a starter.

Sorrel was regarded as an egg herb, and there are a number of ways of serving **Sorrel With Poached Eggs**. In a recipe from the eighteenth century you boil the sorrel, strain well, and keep it warm with plenty of butter. Poach three eggs hard, and three soft, and lay them alternately on the bed of sorrel in a shallow dish. Decorate with fried bread triangles and quartered oranges. Another method is to tie the sorrel in bundles and boil. When tender, cut open the bundles and lay them on a plate with spaces left for large fingers of toast. Lay poached eggs over the toast and sorrel, but allowing some green to show. Pour melted butter over the dish.

A very sharp **Sorrel Dressing** was made by grinding freshly washed leaves with salt and straining off the juice. **Sorrel Sauce**, which was served hot under lamb, veal and sweetbreads, was made by taking a large bundle of the herb, and cooking it with butter over a low heat for about a quarter of an hour. Liquidise, and season with pepper and salt, and a pinch of sugar.

Medicinally it was considered good for the blood, and was used to treat jaundice, liver and kidney complaints, internal ulcers, stings, toothache, and constipation. It was made into a lotion for boils, abscesses, and skin complaints. It was given to animals for fever and skin disorders.

SOUTHERNWOOD (Artemesia abrotanum)

Old Man, or Lad's-love, – in the name there's nothing
To one that knows not Lad's-love, or Old Man,
The hoar-green feathery herb, almost a tree,
Growing with rosemary and lavender.
Even to one that knows it well, the names
Half decorate, half perplex, the thing it is:

At least, what that is clings not to the names
In spite of time. And yet I like the names.

The herb itself I like not, but for certain
I love it, as some day the child will love it
Who plucks a feather from the door-side bush
Whenever she goes in or out of the house.
Often she waits there, snipping the tips and shrivelling
The shreds at last on to the path, perhaps
Thinking, perhaps of nothing, till she sniffs
Her fingers and runs off. The bush is still
But half as tall as she, though it is as old;
So well she clips it. Not a word she says;
And I can only wonder how much hereafter
She will remember, with that bitter scent,
Of garden rows, and ancient damson-trees
Topping a hedge, a bent path to a door,
A low thick bush beside the door, and me
Forbidding her to pick.

As for myself,
Where first I met the bitter scent is lost.
I, too, often shrivel the grey shreds,
Sniff them and think and sniff again and try
Once more to think what it is I am remembering,
Always in vain. I cannot like the scent,
Yet I would rather give up others more sweet,
With no meaning, than this bitter one.

I have mislaid the key. I sniff the spray
And think of nothing; I see and hear nothing;
Yet seem, too, to be listening, lying in wait
For what I should, yet never can, remember:
No garden appears, no path, no hoar-green bush
Of Lad's-love, or Old Man, no child beside,
Neither father nor mother, nor any playmate;
Only an avenue, dark, nameless, without end.

'Old Man' by Edward Thomas.

Unlike Edward Thomas I both love and like southernwood; its delicate feathery 'hoar-green' foliage, and the spicy, bitter scent of the crushed leaves. It is a herb that begs for memories simply because it has been so much the part of the experience of anyone who has lived in and known country gardens all their lives. Like many old plants it has gathered different names, such as Apple-Ringie, Suthwyrt and Sufferingwort. According to William Turner there were male and female southernwoods, but only the female would grow in England.

It was put among clothes and linen to discourage moths, and its ashes were used to encourage hair growth, but in the main it was prescribed as a pain reliever. It was made into a plaster with hot vinegar for pains in the shoulders, wrists and ankles; mixed with oil of roses for muscular aches, while the pounded seeds were soaked in water for sciatica and ruptures, as well as convulsions and poisoning. The herb, which was regarded as an aphrodisiac, was a treatment for hysteria and epilepsy, and cooked with quince or bread, was used to ease inflammation of the eyes.

Animals were given southernwood for worms, digestive problems, kidney, bladder, skin and hair disorders.

SWEET CICELY (Myrrhis odorata)
Its beautiful fine ferny leaves make it a worthwhile plant to include in the herb garden, but, in fact, this stately perennial, which has also been known as Cow Chervil, Fern-leaved Chervil, Sweet Fern, and Giant Sweet Chervil, is very useful in the kitchen. The leaves with their delicate aniseed flavour can be chopped into a salad, and they are excellent cooked with rhubarb, red currants and gooseberries. Because they are sweet, they can, if used plentifully, reduce the amount of sugar used with the fruit.

They go well in salad dressings and cool drinks, and can be added with other fresh herbs to omelettes. Both seeds and leaves bring an interesting flavour to cabbage. In the past the long tap roots were cooked and eaten, and the oily, aromatic seeds were crushed and used as a furniture polish. It was also prescribed for indigestion, either chewing the seeds, or in the form of a tisane.

SWEET WOODRUFF (Asperula odorata)
I have a great fondness for this little woodland plant, that will fit in

anywhere, and makes such a splendid ground cover, with its fresh green leaves, and small white flowers. Because it has the sweet, fresh scent of new mown hay, it was dried and put among linen to freshen it. Garlands of woodruff and lavender were used to decorate and scent churches. Put into summer drinks, especially wine cups, it adds a delicious flavour, and is held to make the drinker feel cheerful and full of well being. Fresh bruised leaves were put on cuts and wounds.

TANSY (Tanacetum vulgare)

Although it does like to take over the entire herb garden given half a chance, it is a plant that must be grown, if only for its gleaming umbels of golden flowers in the late summer. In the past it occupied a very important place, not only in medicine, but also in the diet of the people. It was an essential ingredient in tansies, and was also one of the plants permitted during fast periods. During the spring it was greatly valued as a pick-me-up after the long winter months of a poor, unhealthy diet. Culpeper railed against the Catholic church for limiting the amount that could be eaten at that time of the year, declaring that 'the pope, his imps' and doctors did this deliberately so that people would be ill in the summer and need their services. He also regarded it as a fertility drug, and described it as '. . . their best companion, the husband excepted'.

The herb gave its name to **Tansies**, a dish that was a cross between an omelette and a cake. The young leaves were shredded with other herbs, beaten up with eggs and fried. **Minnow Tansy** was an old spring dish, made from minnows fried with egg yolks, tansy and primroses.

Tansy Pudding, on the other hand, was a great deal more elaborate. 'Boil a quart of cream or milk with a stick of cinnamon, quartered nutmeg, and large mace; when half cold, mix it with twenty yolks of eggs; and ten whites; strain it, then put to it four grated biscuits, half a pound of butter, a pint of spinach juice, and a little tansy, sack and orange flower water, sugar, and a little salt; then gather it to a body over the fire, and pour into your dish, being well buttered; when it is baked, turn it on a pie dish; squeeze on it an orange, grate on sugar, and garnish it with sliced orange and a little tansy.'

Another recipe took more the form of a **Tansy Custard**. 'To make a tansy to bake: take twenty eggs, but eight whites, beat the eggs very well, and strain them into a quart of thick cream, one nutmeg, and three Naples biscuits grated, as much juice of spinach, with a sprig or two of tansy, as will make as green as grass; sweeten it to your taste; then butter your dish very well, and set it into an oven, no hotter than for custards; watch it, as soon as 'tis done, take it out of the oven, and turn it on a pie plate; scrape sugar, and squeeze orange upon it. Garnish the dish with orange and lemon, and serve it up.'

Sometimes fruit was used as a main ingredient. Gooseberries were fried in butter until they became a mash, then 'seven egg yolks and four whites, a pound of sugar, three spoonfuls of sack (sherry), three spoonfuls of cream, a grated penny loaf, and three spoonfuls of flour' were mixed together. The gooseberries were added, and the whole lot thickened in a saucepan before being fried. The finished dish was strewn with sugar and served.

Tansy butter is served with the unique County Cork sausage, the Drisheen, and in the past during hot weather meat was rubbed with tansy to discourage flies.

Distilled tansy water was used to bathe the face to remove pimples, freckles, spots and sunburn. The same effect was sought with tansy infused in white wine or vinegar. The herb was regarded as being good for circulation, and an infusion was drunk or used externally for swellings, sties, bruises, swellings and varicose veins. It was also used to treat jaundice and dropsy, and to stimulate the appetite. The roots were preserved in honey to be taken for gout, and the leaves, which were laid on wounds, were also a strewing herb. Tansy was given to animals for worms, hysteria, fevers and abortion.

TARRAGON (Artemisia dracunculus)

However tricky this herb is to grow, it is always worth persevering, because it is so invaluable in the kitchen. Once known as the Biting Dragon (it was said to be a cure for the bites of dragons), it was chopped into salads to bring a spiciness to the otherwise somewhat bland flavours of lettuce, and less flavoursome salad herbs and vegetables.

It makes an excellent vinegar, which is essential for preparing Sauce Tartare, and is perhaps the most perfect flavouring for chicken. One way is simply to stuff a handful of the fresh leaves into the cavity of the bird, but a more effective **Tarragon Stuffing** is made in the French eighteenth-century manner, which is to parboil the tarragon, squeeze it dry, chop finely and mix with the chopped liver from the fowl and a little butter.

Although it did have a reputation for causing flatulence, it was used as a tonic to clear the head, and tone up the heart and liver.

Russian Tarragon (*Artemisia dracunculoides*) is a very robust plant, that will spread in all directions, but its flavour is so insipid it is simply not worth growing. The one thing that either tarragon loathes is damp. It should be planted in a dry, warm spot, although it really is best to cultivate it in large pots, which can be kept under cover during the winter.

THORN APPLE (Datura stramonium)

This easily raised plant is only to be grown to decorate the herb garden, and because of its long association with the mystical role played by herbs. It has large, distinctive leaves, and handsome white trumpet flowers, followed by huge, thorny seed pods. It is a powerful narcotic, and as such extremely dangerous, and as the Americans, who call it Jimpson Weed, would say, 'don't mess with it'. In some Eastern religions it is used to induce hallucinations. Expert homeopathic practitioners use it to treat asthma. The dried leaves and stalks are smoked to relieve the symptoms. An ointment was made from the leaves for piles. It was also given to animals suffering from asthma and jaundice.

THYME (Thymus vulgaris)

This is without doubt one of the loveliest and most useful of all the herbs, and it would be unthinkable to have a garden without it. Whether it is a sub-shrubby variety, or a dense, mat-forming type, with its neat, dark-green leaves and flowers ranging through shades of red, pink, mauve and white, it is a constant joy. Legend has it that the bed for the baby Jesus in the stable in Bethlehem, was made from thyme. It was burnt as an incense in pagan festivals, and used in charms and incantations, and like parsley, it is one of the herbs to survive the vagaries of taste and fashion.

The Romans included it in a whole range of sauces for boar, boiled ostrich, chicken, mutton, lamb, and with the bulbs they ate for what they fancied to be aphrodisical properties. The Normans served it as a sauce with fish dishes, and traditionally it has been used to flavour hare and sturgeon soups. Mixed with breadcrumbs, it was a coating for meat, especially beef steaks, and fish, before frying or roasting. It remains a favourite ingredient in stuffing for a goose, and in the eighteenth century was mixed with parsley to stuff a leg of lamb, or beef. A sauce for boiled turkey was made with water or stock, a blade of mace, an onion, thyme, a little lemon peel, and an anchovy, which were cooked until tender, liquidised, and mixed with melted butter.

Thyme, which, according to historic advice, should be gathered in flower and dried in the shade, was a strewing herb, and put into baths to sweeten the water. It was, and still is, a valuable bee herb.

Medicinally wild thyme, known as Mother of Thyme, and Brother-wort, was considered the most potent variety. It had a cleansing and disinfectant role, and was made into a poultice for inflammations and surface infections. In the form of an infusion, it was administered as a febrifuge, digestive, a liver tonic, and for headaches, halitosis and hysteria. Epileptics were laid on a bed of thyme during fits. It was believed that the scent of the crushed herb was sufficient to revive them. Doctors prescribed it for lunacy and depression; lung complaints, persistent coughs, and breathing problems, as well as snake bite. A liniment made with oil of roses was rubbed on the forehead and temples to relieve headaches, and a plaster made with vinegar was a treatment for gout and sciatica. Nasal catarrh, noises in the ears, tumours, and a range of gynaecological complaints were doctored with thyme. Animals were given it for digestion, colic, rickets, liver, worms and hysteria.

Apart from the common thyme in its various forms (golden, silver, black and variegated), there are a large number of delightful types, such as the orange-scented *Thymus fragrantissima*, *T. citrodorus*, with its lemon scent, and *T. mastchinus*, which smells of lavender.

Not only does this accommodating herb thrive in herb gardens and borders, but it will grow in pots (inside and out-of-doors), in the cracks in paved and brick paths, in grass paths, and on turf seats.

VALERIAN (Valeriana officinalis)

Dedicated to the Virgin Mary, it was known as the Blessed Herb. It was also called Setwall and Setewale, and was always cultivated in the well-stocked medieval garden. The white and pinky-crimson flowers, and attractive pinnate leaves are a delightful addition to the herb collection. It has always been credited with magical qualities, particularly as a defence against evil and witches. Because its smell was said to attract rats and mice, it was used to bait traps. Medicinally it was used to cure insomnia, and also for the treatment of epilepsy, hysteria, constipation, and worms, as well as bladder, liver and kidney complaints.

WORMWOOD (Artemisia absinthium)

This tall plant, with its bold, grey foliage, is invaluable in border planning, and although it is not long-lived, it seeds itself so freely there is never any lack of replacements. In France it is used in the making of absinthe. A traditional vermifuge, it was additionally employed in the treatment of all digestive problems, including constipation and indigestion. Its ancient name, Wermod, literally translated means 'guard mind', and it was made into a medicine for the mentally ill. Another antique belief was that if the juice of wormwood was rubbed over a baby's hands before it was twelve weeks old it would never suffer extremes of heat or cold during its lifetime. Herbalists also put it to use when dealing with jaundice and kidney troubles; as a plaster for bruises and sprains, and mixed it with honey for bleary eyes. Animals were fed it to perk up a poor appetite, for worms, falling hair, lice, mange, and ear and eye complaints.

Turner wrote of three kinds of wormwood, the best of which, he claimed, was Wormwood Gentle. He also spoke highly of Sea Wormwood (*Artemisia maritima*), which he called Seryphium, from the old Latin name, *Seriphium*. Curiously he said it was only to be found growing in ditches in Northumberland and Norfolk which flooded with sea water. In fact it is pretty common in the south and east of the country, and South Wales.

Epilogue

Palinode:

Is not thilke the mery moneth of May,
When love-lads masken in fresh aray?
How falles it, then, wee no merrier heene,
Ylike as others, girt in gawdy greene?
Our bloncket liveries bene all to sadde
For thilke same season, when all is ycladde
With pleasaunce; the ground with grasse, the woods
With greene leaves, the bushes with bloosming buds.
Youngthes folke now flocken in every where,
To gather May-buskets and smelling brere;
And home they hasten the postes to dight,
And all the kirk-pillours eare day-light,
With hawthorne buds, and sweet eglantine,
And girlonds of roses, and soppes in wine.
Such merimake holy saints doth queme,
But we here sitten as drownde in dreme.

From: 'The Shepeards Calender' (May) by Edmund Spenser.
('Bloncket liveries': grey coats. 'Queme': to please. 'Thilke': the same.)

An epilogue is defined as the concluding part of a literary work, and to conclude is to bring to an end, but I would not wish the reader to imagine that I believe I have had the last word on herbs. With the renewed and growing interest in them in all their different roles, we are going to hear a great deal more about these plants over the next few years.

If it is true that there is nothing new under the sun, then we will be re-learning old knowledge; the wisdom of the ancients and their skills in using herbs. The myths, the magic, and the downright dangerous assertions will be filtered and refined out, although I hope that this often too cynical and pragmatic age will not throw out the many charming legends attached to herbs, and which add so much to their natural beauty.

What has brought about this renaissance of herbs? There are, of course, plenty of good explanations; the expansion of home-ownership and gardening; a greater interest in food and cooking, and an enthusiastic willingness to experiment with an international cuisine. As foreign travel becomes the norm for people from all social and financial backgrounds, so tastes are likely to demand more of the flavours and savours provided by herbs. Already some greengrocers, and the green-grocery departments of the better supermarkets are stocking fresh herbs such as coriander, as well as the ubiquitous parsley and mint. Perhaps the time is not far off when fresh herbs, such as angelica and rue, will be sold from stalls as they were two hundred years ago.

There is another reason, and it is probably the most serious and significant of all: disillusionment. People have become disillusioned with, and in many cases, frightened, by the man-made and the synthetic. This is particularly true of drugs; the appalling, disfiguring effect of Thalidomide, together with the side-effects of cortisone, and steroids, has brought about a desire for a return to more natural methods of treatment, among which herbs occupy a dominant position.

The irony is that the very medicines that people fear originate from plants, but by isolating, and then synthesizing, the essential elements in a plant, the effect on a patient is so much greater than when the cure is given in the simple, old-fashioned way, unadulterated by the laboratory. Of course, it would be quite wrong to dismiss all advances in medicine as dangerous and capricious, but what is emerging is a desire to combine the best of traditional and modern medicine. The Chinese appear to have been quite remarkably successful in this approach by merging acupuncture and herbalism, with the most advanced techniques of surgery and treatment. Homeopathy and Naturopathy, once regarded as the exclusive dotty province of cranks and faddists, and many other branches of fringe medicine, are not only becoming increasingly accepted by growing numbers of people, but are also seen to be useful by the medical profession.

The dislike of synthetic, or so called man-made products, extends to food, with its artificial flavouring and colouring; chemical dyes, and the use of chemical fertilisers, herbicides, insecticides, and fungicides, to boost production and grow uniform crops to meet the demands of food processors. Organic farming and market gardening, like alternative medicine, has now earned a new respectability, and the serious support of both consumers, producers and retailers.

The interest in conservation and the will to attempt to reverse the trend that has led to the destruction, or near destruction, of so many of our lovely native plants, has given a new lease for many of the herbs, or simples, that used to be collected from the meadows, woods and roadsides. What were regarded as no more than noxious weeds, are being given a place in the garden, and as a consequence are very likely to come back into use in tisanes and tonics, or perhaps just to attract butterflies and other insects which have been put at risk by methods of intensive cultivation. In fact utilitarianism is not really all that important if the movement in favour of herbs preserves this enchanting part of our inheritance.

Instead of sitting 'drowned in dream', how much better it would be if our 'young folk', as in Spenser's day could fill great baskets with roses, honeysuckle, carnations and pinks, and all the other sweetly scented and useful herbs that would please the holy saints, without worrying whether or not they might become extinct.

One certain way of securing the future of herbs is for every gardener to make sure that they give some space to them; not out of a sense of duty, but so that they can enjoy these glorious and rewarding plants.

Bibliography

Bardswell, Frances A., *The Herb Garden*, A & C Black Ltd., 1930.

Beeton, Mrs. Isabella, *The Book of Household Management*, S. O. Beeton, 1864.

Bey, Pilaff (Edited by Norman Douglas), *Venus in the Kitchen, or Love's Cookery Book*, William Heinemann Ltd., 1952.

Blomfield, Reginald, *The Formal Garden in England*, Waterstone, 1985.

Bowles, E. A., *A Handbook of the Narcissus*, Waterstone, 1985.

Brownlow, Margaret, *The Delights of Herb-Growing*, The Herb Farm Ltd., 1966.

Burton, Robert, *The Anatomy of Melancholy* (Edited by the Rev. A. R. Shilleto), G. Bell and Sons, 1920.

Clarkson, Rosetta E., *Herbs: Their Culture and Uses*, The Macmillan Company (New York), 1942.

Conway, David, *The Magic of Herbs*, Jonathan Cape, 1973.

Crisp, Sir Frank, *Medieval Gardens*, John Lane, 1924.

Culpeper, Nicholas, *Culpeper's Complete Herbal & English Physician*, 1826.

Dioscorides, *The Greek Herbal of*, Englished by John Goodyer, 1655 (Edited and first printed by Robert T. Gunther, Oxford University Press, 1934).

Evelyn, John, *Acetaria. A Discourse on Sallets*, 1699.

Fitzherbert, Master, *The Book of Husbandry*, 1534.

Flint, Martha Bockee, *A Garden of Simples*, David Nutt, 1901.

Flower, B. and Hosenbaum, E., *Apicius: The Roman Cookery Book. A*

Critical Translation of the Art of Cooking, 1958.

Frazer, Mrs., *The Practice of Cookery*. Printed for Peter Hill by J. Ruthven and Sons, 1800.

Gardener, Master John (Edited by the Hon. A. M. T. Amherst), *The Feate of Gardening*, 1894.

Gerarde, John, *The Herbal or General Historie of Plantes Gathered by John Gerarde of London*, Master in Chirurgerie, 1597.

Glasse, Mrs. Hannah, *The Art of Cookery Made Plain and Easy*, 1775.

Grigson, Geoffrey, *A Herbal of all Sorts*, Phoenix House, 1959.

Harding, Alice, *The Book of the Peony*, Waterstone, 1985.

Harvey, John, *Medieval Gardens*, Batsford, 1981.

Jekyll, Gertrude, *Children and Gardens*, Country Life, 1933.

Johns, Rev. C. J., *Flowers of the Field*, George Routledge & Sons Ltd., 1913.

Kitchiner, Dr. William, *The Cook's Oracle*, Robert Cadell, 1840.

Kreig, Margaret B., *Green Medicine*, George G. Harrap & Co. Ltd., 1965.

Levy, Juliette de Bairacli, *Herbal Handbook for Farm and Stable*, Faber and Faber, 1952.

Leyel, Mrs. C. F. (H.W), *Cinquefoil: Herbs to Quicken the Five Senses*, Faber and Faber, 1957.

Leyel, Mrs. C. F. (H.W), *Green Medicine*, Faber and Faber, 1952.

Lyte, Charles, *The Kitchen Garden*, The Oxford Illustrated Press, 1984.

Martin, W. Keble, *The Concise British Flora*, Ebury Press and Michael Joseph, 1969.

Mead, William Edward, *The English Medieval Feast*, George Allen & Unwin, 1931.

Parkinson, John, *Paradisi in Sole, Parradisus Terrestris*, 1629.

Parkinson, John, *Theatrum Botanicum*, 1640.

Pliny, *Natural History of the World, Commonly called, The Natural Historie of C. Plinius Secundus* (Pliny the Elder), Translated into English by Philemon Holland, Doctor of Physicke, 1634.

Redgrove, H. S., *Spices and Condiments*, Sir Isaac Pitman & Sons Ltd., 1933.

Rohde, Eleanour Sinclair, *A Garden of Herbs*.

Smith, Elizabeth, *The Compleat Housewife* or *Accomplish'd Gentlewoman's Companion*, 1744.

Tudor, Alice M., *A Little Book of Healing Herbs: Gathered from an old Herbal*, The Medici Society, 1927.

Turner, William, *The Names of Herbes* (1548), Published for the English Dialect Society by N. Trubner & Co., 1881.

Ward, Elizabeth, *The French Family Cook*, 1793.

Wheaton, Barbara Ketcham, *Savouring the Past: The French Kitchen and Table from 1300 to 1789*, Chatto and Windus, 1983.

Wright, Richardson, *The Story of Gardening from the Hanging Gardens of Babylon to the Hanging Gardens of New York*, George Routledge and Sons Ltd., 1934.

Index

Index

Index